OED

I0120174

INDIA: THE CHALLENGES OF DEVELOPMENT

A Country Assistance Evaluation

Gianni Zanini

2001
The World Bank
Washington, D.C.

http://www.worldbank.org/html/oed

ACKNOWLEDGMENTS

This Country Assistance Evaluation (CAE) builds on evaluations of sector assistance programs, projects, and nonlending services to assess the development effectiveness of Bank assistance to India during the 1990s. It uses the Operations Evaluation Department's (OED) standard evaluation categories: outcome (that is, relevance, efficacy, and efficiency), sustainability, and institutional development.

The areas covered by the evaluation work broadly mirror those emphasized in the Country Assistance Strategy (CAS) documents of the late 1990s. They reflect the main assessment categories of country performance proposed in the replenishment paper for IDA12 and are generally consistent with the comprehensive development framework: private and financial sector development; public sector management reform; rural and urban development; energy, water management, and transport; human and social development; and the environment.

Reviewers who commented on early drafts (but who cannot be held responsible for errors, omissions, or for OED's evaluation judgments) include, among current or former World Bank staff, Mark Baird, country director for Indonesia, East Asia and Pacific Region (EAP); Vinay Bhargava, country director for the Philippines, EAP; Pieter Bottelier, consultant (former country director for China, EAP); Sarwar Lateef, senior adviser, Poverty Reduction and Economic Management Network; Martin Ravallion, lead adviser on poverty, Development Economics and Chief Economist (DEC); Anandarup Ray, consultant (former senior economic adviser, DEC); Daniel Ritchie, consultant (former director for the Asia Technical Department); and Anwar Shah, principal evaluator and public sector management cluster leader, OED. Outside reviewers include Marc Lindenberg, Dean, Graduate School of Public Affairs, University of Washington (former Senior Vice-President, CARE) and the following Indian experts: S. Aiyar, U.S.-based correspondent, *Economic Times* of India; R. Mohan, Director, National Council of Applied Economic Research, New Delhi; G. Sen, Professor, Indian Institute of Management, Bangalore, and Chair of the External Gender Consultative Group, World Bank; A. Sengupta, Professor, J.N. University, New Delhi, (former member of the Planning Commission and Executive Director, International Monetary Fund); T. N. Srinivasan, Professor, Economics Department, Yale University; and Isher J. Ahluwalia, Director and Chief Executive, Indian Council for Research on International Economic Relations, New Delhi, who also provided feedback on early drafts of the background papers dealing with poverty and core macroeconomic issues.

Bank staff and Indian officials and observers were interviewed during 1999 and 2000 in Washington, D.C., and in India. During a CAE mission in April and May 1999, which included visits to Ahmedabad, Delhi, Hyderabad, Lucknow, and Mumbai, group discussions were held in Delhi on a number of sectoral topics and cross-cutting themes. Further sectoral consultations and joint CAE/CAS workshops (jointly organized by OED and the South Asia Region) took place from March to May 2000 (for health and forestry in 1999). In April 2000, a second CAE mission held final consultations on a preliminary CAE draft and a CAE/CAS synthesis workshop (also joint with the Region).

Various background papers and notes were prepared by consultants and OED staff and are available as part of the OED Working Paper Series. They all have taken into account comments received from peer reviewers, Bank staff, civil society, and the government. Their findings, however, remain entirely the responsibility of the individual authors. These papers are available on request.

The core team members produced evaluative papers in their areas of responsibility: Dinanath Khatkhate, on private sector and financial sector development; Jack van Holst Pellekaan, on rural development and on poverty; and Baran Tuncer, on public sector management and state focus. Other contributors included: Swaminathan Aiyar (consultant) on the Bank's external communications strategy; Anaya Basu (Development Economics Research Group, World Bank) on gender; Helen Abadzi (Operations Evaluation Department Sector and Thematic Evaluation, OEDST, World Bank), Sukhdeep Brar, and Aklilu Habte (consultants) on education; Hernan Levy (OEDST, World Bank) on transport; Om Prakash Mathur (consultant) on urban development; T. N. Srinivasan (consultant) on economic challenges for poverty reduction and growth; A. Vaidyanathan (consultant) on irrigation (this paper was used as an input to the rural development and the water resource management background papers); Warren Van Wicklin III (Operations Evaluation Department Corporate Evaluation and Methods, World Bank) on social development; and Vinod Sahgal and Deepa Chakrapani (OEDCM) on public financial accountability.

The CAE also relied on various ongoing OED sector assistance reviews (which were also case studies for Bankwide sector assistance reviews): by R. Berney and J. Levine (OEDST) on energy; Uma Lele (OEDST) and N. Kumar (consultant) on forestry; Keith Pitman (OEDST) and I. J. Singh (consultant) on water resource management; R. Ridker (consultant) and S. Stout (Operations Evaluation Department Office of the Director) on health, nutrition, and population; and K. Ringskog (OEDST) and Nola Chow (consultant) on environment. Also, Rema Balasundaram and Patricia Laverley (OEDPK) reviewed the lessons from other donors' evaluations and Barbara Yale (OEDCM) analyzed the aid coordination survey. Finally, the CAE and some of the background papers drew on recent OED and Quality Assurance Group evaluations on the dairy industry, NGOs, resettlement, rural water supply, and sanitation.

Stephen Howes and Mandakini Kaul of the New Delhi Office (among other staff) and Chitra Bhanu (OED consultant) were instrumental in the organization of the extensive consultations held in March–May 2000 and in coordinating all the comments required of regional staff on the many background papers.

J. Gwyer and O. Rajakaruna (consultants) provided inputs on portfolio management and performance, quality at entry, and research and gave statistical assistance. W. Hurlbut (OEDST) provided editorial advice. R. Baba, N. Namisato, C. Diaw, and D. Flex invaluably supported the entire CAE team.

Gianni Zanini (task manager, Operations Evaluation Department Country Evaluation and Regional Relations) produced the main CAE report with close assistance from Jack van Holst Pellekaan (consultant). The main report has taken into account comments from the reviewers mentioned above, OED staff and management, former and current Bank staff and management working on India, and former and current officials in the Government of India. Official government comments on the October 24, 2000, draft of the CAE were received only from the Ministry of Human Resource Development. Those comments were taken into account in preparing this version of the CAE and are discussed in the background paper titled "Evaluating Bank Assistance for Education Sector Development."

The study was published in the Partnerships and Knowledge Group (OEDPK) by the Outreach and Dissemination Unit. The task team includes Elizabeth Campbell-Pagé (task team leader), Caroline McEuen (editor), and Juicy Qureishi-Huq (administrative assistant).

Director-General, Operations Evaluation Department:
Robert Picciotto
Director, Operations Evaluation Department:
Gregory K. Ingram
Manager, Country Evaluation & Regional Relations:
Ruben Lamdany
Task Manager: *Gianni Zanini*

FOREWORD

ENGLISH

This evaluation assesses the development effectiveness of Bank assistance to India during the 1990s. India was one of the Bank's founding members and remains one of its largest and most influential borrowers. The Bank has been India's largest source of external long-term capital and has financed a sizable share of its public investment. Its lending and nonlending services have been thinly spread over many central and state agencies and have addressed many different objectives.

India entered the decade with substantial economic and social achievements but also with closed trade and investment regimes, fiscal imbalances, and a large and unwieldy public sector. After a balance of payments crisis in 1991 it deregulated the trade and investment regimes. Economic growth rebounded quickly and proved resilient even during the 1997 East Asian crisis. Social indicators also improved. India, however, failed to sustain the reform process in the fiscal area and to broaden it to other structural areas. Moreover, there was little progress in reducing rural poverty, largely due to the absence of an effective agricultural and rural development strategy and low growth in the poorer northern and eastern states. In the second half of the 1990s, a few states initiated substantial policy and institutional changes, but there remains a large outstanding reform agenda at both the state and federal levels.

PRÓLOGO

ESPAÑOL

En este documento se evalúa la eficacia de la asistencia prestada por el Banco a la India en los años noventa con el propósito de impulsar el proceso de desarrollo de ese país. La India, miembro fundador del Banco, sigue siendo uno de sus prestatarios más grandes e influyentes. El Banco ha sido el mayor proveedor externo de capital a largo plazo del país y ha financiado una proporción considerable de las inversiones del sector público; asimismo, ha suministrado servicios crediticios y no crediticios, con objetivos muy diversos, a numerosos organismos del gobierno central y de los estados.

La India comenzó el decenio con notables logros económicos y sociales, pero también con regímenes cerrados de comercio e inversiones, desequilibrios fiscales y un sector público grande e inmanejable. Tras la crisis de balanza de pagos de 1991, desreguló dichos regímenes. El crecimiento económico se recuperó rápidamente y resistió, incluso, los embates de la crisis que sacudió al este asiático en 1997. También los indicadores sociales mejoraron. Sin embargo, la India no consiguió mantener el proceso de reformas en el campo fiscal ni ampliarlo a otros sectores estructurales. Además, la pobreza se redujo muy poco en las zonas rurales, en gran medida debido a la ausencia de una estrategia eficaz de desarrollo agrícola y rural y al escaso crecimiento de los estados más pobres del norte y el este. En la segunda mitad del decenio de 1990, algunos estados emprendieron importantes reformas normativas e institu-

PREFACE

FRANÇAIS

Cette étude évalue l'efficacité de l'assistance de la Banque au développement de l'Inde pendant les années 1990. L'Inde est l'un des membres fondateurs de la Banque est reste l'un de ses emprunteurs les plus importants et les plus influents. La Banque est la principale source de capitaux extérieurs à long terme du pays et finance une part notable de ses investissements publics. Ses prêts et ses activités non financières concernent une multitude d'agences des états et du gouvernement fédéral et poursuivent un grand nombre d'objectifs divers.

Au début des années 1990, l'Inde avait déjà fait d'importants progrès sur le plan économique et social, mais son développement était freiné par des réglementations restrictives en matière de commerce et d'investissement, par les déficits budgétaires et par la taille et la lourdeur du secteur public. À la suite d'une crise de la balance des paiements en 1991, le gouvernement a libéralisé le commerce et les investissements. La relance économique a été rapide et a résisté à la crise qui a frappé l'Asie Orientale en 1997. Les indicateurs sociaux se sont améliorés. Cependant, l'Inde n'a pas réussi à maintenir le rythme des réformes budgétaires et à étendre le processus à d'autres problèmes structurels. En outre, peu de progrès ont été faits vers une réduction de la pauvreté rurale, en l'absence d'une stratégie agricole et de développement rural efficace et du fait de la faible croissance des états les plus pauvres du nord et de l'est.

ENGLISH

The Bank provided strong support for the reforms of the early 1990s, beginning with three adjustment loans. It expanded assistance to the social sectors; devoted more attention to improving participation; and, where development results had been unsatisfactory, reduced lending (to virtually zero in power) and embarked on comprehensive sector work—for example, in rural development and irrigation. After the mid-1990s the Bank focused assistance on reforming states, with a notable measure of success. Still, more emphasis on fiscal management, on public sector and judicial reforms, on improvement in agricultural policies and rural development, and on gender equity may have led to greater impact.

Overall, the strategic goals of the Bank were relevant and the design of the assistance strategy improved as the decade unfolded. Efficacy was modest, mainly on account of the Bank's limited impact on fiscal and other structural reforms, the failure to develop an effective assistance strategy for rural poverty reduction, and the mediocre quality at exit of projects. Institutional development impact has also been modest and sustainability uncertain given the remaining serious fiscal imbalances, high environmental costs, and governance weaknesses. Thus, the overall outcome of the assistance for the decade is rated as moderately satisfactory.

The relevance of the assistance strategy, however, has improved substantially over the past two years through a more sharpened focus on poverty reduction, a more selective approach to state assistance, and

ESPAÑOL

cionales, pero son muchos los cambios pendientes, tanto en el gobierno federal como en los estados.

El Banco proporcionó un fuerte respaldo para las reformas de principios de los años noventa, comenzando con tres préstamos para fines de ajuste. Amplió su asistencia a los sectores sociales; dedicó mayor atención a mejorar la participación; y, donde los resultados no habían sido satisfactorios en términos de desarrollo, redujo el financiamiento (prácticamente a cero para el sector de la energía) e inició amplios estudios sectoriales, por ejemplo, en la esfera del riego y el desarrollo rural. En la segunda mitad del decenio, el Banco centró su asistencia en la reforma de los estados, con bastante éxito. No obstante, se podrían haber logrado mejores resultados si se hubiera hecho más hincapié en la administración fiscal, la reforma del sector público y el poder judicial, el mejoramiento de las políticas agrícolas y el desarrollo rural, y la igualdad entre los géneros.

En general, los objetivos estratégicos del Banco fueron pertinentes y el diseño de la estrategia de asistencia fue mejorando a medida que avanzaba el decenio. La eficacia resultó moderada, fundamentalmente debido a la limitada incidencia del Banco en las reformas fiscales y otras reformas estructurales, la incapacidad para elaborar una estrategia de asistencia eficaz para reducir la pobreza en las zonas rurales y la mediocre calidad final de los proyectos. Los efectos para el desarrollo institucional también han sido escasos y la sostenibilidad, incierta, en vista de los graves desequilibrios fiscales que aún existen, los elevados costos ambientales y las deficiencias de la gestión pública.

FRANÇAIS

Pendant la deuxième moitié des années 1990, quelques états ont commencé à réformer leurs politiques et leurs institutions; néanmoins, c'est un vaste programme de réformes que l'Inde doit encore entreprendre au niveau des états et du gouvernement fédéral.

Au début des années 1990, la Banque a fortement soutenu les réformes, au moyen tout d'abord de trois prêts d'ajustement. Elle a ensuite étendu son assistance aux secteurs sociaux et a accordé une attention particulière à une meilleur participation; là où les résultats obtenus étaient décevants, elle a réduit ses prêts (à virtuellement zéro dans le secteur de l'énergie), mais a entrepris un vaste programme d'études sectorielles, par exemple dans le développement rural et l'irrigation. Depuis le milieu des années 1990, la Banque a concentré avec succès son assistance sur les états réformateurs. Néanmoins, l'aide de la Banque aurait peut-être été plus efficace si l'institution avait accordé une plus haute priorité à la gestion budgétaire, à la réforme du secteur public et du pouvoir judiciaire, à l'amélioration des politiques agricoles et de développement rural et à l'égalité des sexes.

Ce document a une distribution restreinte et ne peut être utilisé par ses destinataires que dans l'exercice de leurs fonctions officielles. Son contenu ne peut être divulgué qu'avec l'autorisation de la Banque Mondiale.

Dans l'ensemble, les objectifs stratégiques de la Banque étaient sains et la structure de la stratégie d'assistance s'est améliorée tout au long de la décennie. Le programme a eu une efficacité modeste, du fait surtout de l'influence limitée de la Banque sur la réforme budgétaire et d'autres réformes structurelles, de son

ENGLISH

greater attention to governance and institutions. But it is too early to gauge the efficacy of these recent initiatives.

India has built strong foundations for development. The Bank's main challenge is to support far-reaching reforms, at both the state and central government levels, with high-quality and widely disseminated policy studies and policy-based sector and program loans. The five pillars and the fiscal and structural reform triggers of the 1997 Country Assistance Strategy remain valid. Thus, only adjustments to accelerate and assure the full application of those pillars and triggers appear necessary.

The Bank should link the overall lending volumes to fiscal discipline at the central government level and to progress in structural reforms in agriculture and the implementation of an effective rural development strategy, as progress in these areas is crucial for rural poverty reduction. New lending should be concentrated in reforming states, where an assistance strategy has been agreed with the state government, while maintaining a strong policy dialogue with the center and supporting analyses of state finances, policies, and institutions in nonreforming states. Similarly, sectoral lending volumes should be linked to agreements on sector-specific policies and institutional frameworks.

While in recent years Bank assistance has become more pro-poor, the Bank should make greater efforts to monitor systematically the poverty and gender impacts of Bank-assisted projects and programs, as well as to mainstream gender beyond the social sectors. It should also assist government agencies to do the

ESPAÑOL

En consecuencia, el resultado general de la ayuda prestada durante el decenio en su conjunto se califica como moderadamente satisfactoria.

Sin embargo, la pertinencia de la estrategia de asistencia ha mejorado considerablemente en los últimos dos años, gracias a una dedicación especial a la reducción de la pobreza, un criterio más selectivo frente a la ayuda a los estados y una mayor atención a la gestión de gobierno y las instituciones. Pero todavía es demasiado pronto para evaluar la eficacia de estas iniciativas recientes.

La India también ha sentado bases sólidas para el desarrollo. La principal dificultad, para el Banco, consiste en respaldar reformas profundas, tanto en los estados como en el gobierno central, con estudios sobre políticas, de excelente calidad y amplia difusión, y préstamos para programas y reformas de políticas sectoriales. Los cinco pilares y los mecanismos de activación de la reforma fiscal y estructural establecidos en la estrategia de asistencia al país de 1997 siguen siendo válidos. Por ello, sólo parecen ser necesarios los ajustes destinados a acelerar y asegurar la plena aplicación de dichos pilares y mecanismos.

El Banco debería condicionar el volumen global del financiamiento a la disciplina fiscal del gobierno central, así como al avance de las reformas estructurales en el sector agrícola y la ejecución de una estrategia eficaz de desarrollo rural, puesto que el progreso en estos campos es crucial para reducir la pobreza en las zonas rurales. Los nuevos préstamos deberían concentrarse en la reforma de los estados con cuyas autoridades se hubiera acordado una nueva estrategia de asistencia, a la vez que se

FRANÇAIS

incapacité de mettre au point une stratégie efficace de réduction de la pauvreté rurale et de la qualité médiocre des projets achevés. L'impact de la Banque sur le développement institutionnel a également été modeste et la durabilité des effets de ses interventions est incertaine, compte tenu de l'importance des déficits budgétaires, de graves problèmes d'environnement et d'une faible gouvernance. Bref, les résultats globaux de cette assistance pendant l'ensemble de la décennie sont considérés comme modérément satisfaisants.

Néanmoins, la pertinence de la stratégie s'est nettement améliorée au cours des deux dernières années, du fait d'une plus grande concentration sur la réduction de la pauvreté, d'une aide plus sélective aux états et d'une attention plus forte aux problèmes de gouvernance et de développement institutionnel. Toutefois, il est encore trop tôt pour évaluer l'efficacité de ces nouvelles initiatives.

L'Inde a bâti de solides fondations pour son développement futur. Pour la Banque, le principal défi est d'appuyer de profondes réformes au niveau des états et du gouvernement fédéral, grâce à des études de haute qualité largement disséminées et à des prêts programmes et des prêts sectoriels pour la réforme des politiques. Les cinq principales composantes du document de stratégie de 1997 et les conditions relatives à la réforme budgétaire et aux réformes structurelles restent valables. Seuls quelques ajustements paraissent nécessaires pour accélérer et renforcer l'exécution des composantes et des conditions.

La Banque doit lier le volume global de ses prêts à la discipline

ENGLISH

same for overall public expenditure programs. Finally, it should strengthen aid coordination on country assistance strategies and on critical sector strategies (for example, agriculture and rural development) to enhance the effectiveness of external assistance and enable greater selectivity in the Bank's own programs.

ESPAÑOL

mantiene un intenso diálogo sobre políticas con el gobierno central y se respaldan los análisis de las finanzas, políticas e instituciones de los estados que no han iniciado reformas. Análogamente, los volúmenes de financiamiento sectorial deberían vincularse a acuerdos sobre marcos normativos e institucionales propios de cada sector.

Aun cuando en los últimos años la asistencia del Banco se ha orientado más a reducir la pobreza, el Banco debería desplegar mayores esfuerzos para realizar un seguimiento sistemático de los efectos de los proyectos y programas que financia en la pobreza y en la situación de la mujer, así como para incorporar la problemática del género a otros sectores, además de los sociales. Debería, asimismo, ayudar a los organismos públicos a hacer lo mismo en relación con los programas globales de gasto público. Por último, debería mejorar la coordinación de la ayuda en las estrategias de asistencia al país y en las estrategias para sectores de importancia crítica (como la agricultura y el desarrollo rural) a fin de mejorar la eficacia de la asistencia externa y permitir una mayor selectividad en los propios programas del Banco.

FRANÇAIS

budgétaire au niveau du gouvernement central, au progrès des réformes structurelles dans l'agriculture et à la mise en œuvre d'une stratégie efficace de développement rural; en effet, des progrès dans ces domaines sont essentiels pour la réduction de la pauvreté rurale. Les prêts nouveaux doivent être concentrés sur les états réformateurs, sur la base d'un accord sur la stratégie d'assistance avec chaque gouvernement; dans les états qui refusent les réformes, la Banque doit maintenir un bon dialogue de politiques et appuyer des études de la situation financièr, des politiques et des institutions des états. De la même façon, le volume des prêts sectoriels doit être lié à des accords précis sur les politiques et les institutions du secteur.

Au cours des dernières années, l'assistance de la Banque à été de plus en plus orientée sur les problèmes de pauvreté; néanmoins, la Banque doit intensifier ses efforts pour organiser un suivi systématique de l'impact de ses programmes et projets sur la pauvreté et la condition féminine; elle doit aussi intégrer les problèmes d'égalité des sexes dans l'ensemble de ses opérations, au delà des seuls secteurs sociaux. La Banque doit aussi aider les agences gouvernementales a étendre cette pratique aux programmes de dépenses publiques. Enfin, elle doit renforcer la coordination des stratégies d'assistance des bailleurs de fonds et des stratégies sectorielles pour les secteurs critiques (par exemple l'agriculture et le développement rural), afin d'améliorer l'efficacité de l'aide extérieure et d'accroître la sélectivité de ses propres programmes.

Robert Picciotto
Director-General, Operations Evaluation

EXECUTIVE SUMMARY

India was one of the Bank's founding members. It is still one of the Bank's main borrowers and has had a major influence on the Bank's understanding of development. The Bank has been India's largest source of external capital, providing almost a third of all long-term gross inflows in the 1980s and more than a fifth by the end of the 1990s.

With more than a quarter (more than 300 million) of the world's poor, India's performance is critical to the achievement of the International Development Goals, which include halving poverty worldwide between 1990 and 2015. This evaluation assesses the development effectiveness of Bank assistance to India during the 1990s.

A Large, Unfinished Reform Agenda

India entered the 1990s with a substantial record of achievement. Famine had been eradicated and self-sufficiency in food production achieved. Social indicators had improved, with a rise in life expectancy, a reduction in infant mortality, a moderated population growth rate, and increased primary school enrollment. But these indicators trailed those of China and many other low-income countries, and India ranks 132 out of 174 countries on the Human Development Index. At the same time, only modest steps had been taken toward economic reform, and India trailed in global economic competition as well, burdened with

RÉSUMEN

La India fue uno de los miembros fundadores del Banco. Es todavía uno de sus principales prestatarios y ha tenido una gran influencia en la manera en que el Banco entiende el desarrollo. El Banco ha sido la mayor fuente de capital externo de la India, ya que ha suministrado casi un tercio de todas las entradas brutas a largo plazo en el decenio de 1980, y más de una quinta parte al final de los años noventa.

Lo que ocurra en la India, país donde se concentra una cuarta parte (más de 300 millones) de los pobres de todo el mundo, es de gran trascendencia para el logro de las metas internacionales de desarrollo, entre las que se incluye reducir la pobreza mundial a la mitad entre 1990 y 2015. En la presente evaluación se intentará calibrar la eficacia en términos de desarrollo de la asistencia del Banco a la India durante el decenio de 1990.

Un programa de reforma ambicioso e inacabado

La India comenzó el decenio de 1990 con un historial bastante positivo. Se había erradicado el hambre y se había alcanzado la autosuficiencia en la producción de alimentos. Los indicadores sociales habían mejorado: alta esperanza de vida, reducción de la mortalidad infantil, moderada tasa de crecimiento demográfico y aumento de la matrícula escolar primaria. Pero estos indicadores iban a la zaga de los de

RÉSUMÉ ANALYTIQUE

L'Inde est l'un des membres fondateurs de la Banque. Le pays, qui est resté l'un des plus grands emprunteurs de l'institution, a beaucoup influencé les conceptions de la Banque en matière de développement. La Banque est la principale source de capitaux étrangers de l'Inde; ses financements, qui dans les années 1980 représentaient près du tiers des apports bruts de capitaux, dépassaient encore le cinquième de ces apports vers la fin des années 1990.

La performance d'un pays qui compte plus du quart des pauvres du monde (plus de 300 millions) est d'une importance critique pour l'accomplissement des Objectifs du Développement International, qui visent notamment à réduire de moitié la pauvreté dans le monde de 1990 à 2015. La présente évaluation étudie l'efficacité de l'assistance de la Banque au développement de l'Inde pendant les années 1990.

Un Vaste Programme de Réformes, Encore Inachevé

Au début des années 1990, l'Inde avait déjà derrière elle d'importantses réalisations. La famine avait été éradiquée et le pays était parvenu au stade de l'auto-suffisance alimentaire. Les indicateurs sociaux s'étaient améliorés, grâce à l'allongement de l'espérance de vie, à la réduction de la mortalité infantile, à une modération de la croissance démographique et à l'augmentation des taux de scolarisation primaire. Néanmoins ces indicateurs étaient encore

ENGLISH

closed trade and investment regimes, fiscal imbalances, and a large and unwieldy public sector.

A balance of payments crisis in 1991 prompted policymakers to move toward reform. The approach was designed to give the private sector a greater role in India's development by improving the investment and tax regimes, reorienting foreign investment policy, opening infrastructure to private investment, reforming public enterprises and the financial sector, and reducing price controls. The reforms paid off: economic growth rebounded and proved resilient, even during the East Asian crisis of 1997. But India failed to sustain the fiscal reform process and to broaden it to other structural areas. There has also been little progress in addressing rural poverty, largely because of the lack of an effective agricultural and rural development strategy and low growth in the poorer northern and eastern states. In the second half of the 1990s, a few states initiated substantial policy and institutional changes, but there is a large outstanding reform agenda at both the state and the federal levels.

The Banks' Approach in the 1990s: Enhanced Relevance

The relevance of Bank assistance increased markedly during and immediately after the 1990–91 macroeconomic crisis. During the first half of the 1990s, the Bank focused on crucial areas of reform for sustainable growth for improved macroeconomic management and liberalization of the trade and investment regimes and on human development for broadbased improvement in primary social

ESPAÑOL

China y muchos otros países de ingreso bajo, y la India ocupa el número 132 entre un total de 174 en lo que se refiere al índice de desarrollo humano. Al mismo tiempo, se habían conseguido sólo modestos progresos hacia la reforma económica, y la India era menos competitiva a escala mundial, sobrecargada como estaba con unos regímenes cerrados de comercio e inversión, desequilibrios fiscales y un sector público muy grande y poco manejable.

La crisis de la balanza de pagos de 1991 impulsó a las autoridades a promover la reforma. El objetivo era dar al sector privado un papel más importante en el desarrollo de la India, mejorando los regímenes de inversión e impuestos, reorientando la política de inversión externa, abriendo la infraestructura a la inversión privada, reformando las empresas públicas del sector financiero y reduciendo los controles de precios. Las reformas dieron resultado: el crecimiento económico se reanimó y demostró su capacidad de resistencia, incluso durante la crisis de Asia oriental de 1997. No obstante, la India no logró sostener el proceso de reforma fiscal ni ampliarlo a otras áreas estructurales. Además, se había progresado poco en la lucha contra la pobreza rural, en buena parte por falta de una estrategia agrícola y de desarrollo rural eficaz y por el bajo crecimiento de los estados más pobres del norte y del este. En la segunda mitad el decenio de 1990, algunos estados iniciaron considerables cambios normativos e institucionales, pero todavía hay un amplio programa de reforma pendiente tanto en el plano federal como estatal.

FRANÇAIS

inférieurs à ceux de la Chine et de beaucoup d'autres pays à faible revenu. L'Indice du Développement Humain place l'Inde au 132ème rang sur un total de 174 pays. En outre, seuls des progrès modestes avaient été accomplis vers les réformes économiques et l'Inde – pénalisée par des réglementations restrictives en matière de commerce et d'investissement, par ses déficits budgétaires et par la taille et la lourdeur de son secteur public – était loin derrière beaucoup d'autres sur le plan de la compétitivité économique.

Une crise de la balance des paiements en 1991 a poussé les dirigeants du pays à s'engager dans la voie des réformes. Il s'agissait d'accorder une place plus importante au secteur privé dans le développement de l'Inde, en réformant le régime fiscal et la réglementation des investissements, en révisant les politiques concernant les investissements étrangers, en ouvrant le secteur des infrastructures à l'investissement privé, en restructurant les entreprises publiques et le secteur financier et en assouplissant le contrôle des prix. Les réformes ont donné de bons résultats: la relance de la croissance économique a persisté et même résisté à la crise qui a frappé l'Asie Orientale en 1997. Cependant, l'Inde n'a pas mis en oeuvre un programme de réforme budgétaire et n'a pas étendu le train des réformes à d'autres problèmes structurels. Peu de progrès ont été réalisés dans le domaine de la pauvreté rurale, pour deux raisons principales: l'absence d'une stratégie agricole et de développement rural efficace et le faible croissance des états les plus pauvres du nord et de

ENGLISH

services. It also expanded support for environmental protection and devoted more attention to improving participation. Where development results were unsatisfactory, the Bank reduced lending (to virtually zero in power) and launched comprehensive sector work.

In the second half of the 1990s, and most notably after 1997, the relevance of Bank assistance to poverty reduction improved. In the mid-1990s, the Bank began to focus assistance on reforming states, with notable success. But greater emphasis on fiscal management, public sector and judicial reform, agricultural policy and rural development, and gender equity would have been beneficial.

Overall, the strategic goals of the Bank during the decade were relevant and the design of the assistance strategy improved. Efficacy is rated as modest, mainly because of the Bank's limited impact on fiscal and other structural reforms, the failure to develop an effective assistance strategy for rural poverty reduction, and the mediocre quality of projects at exit. Institutional development impact has also been modest, and sustainability uncertain, given the serious remaining fiscal imbalances, high environmental costs, and governance weaknesses. Taken together, these ratings gauge the overall outcome of assistance for the decade as moderately satisfactory.

But these ratings must be viewed in light of the recent, substantial improvement in the relevance of the assistance strategy, largely prompted by the innovations embodied in the 1997 Country Assistance Strategy (CAS). The focus on

ESPAÑOL

El enfoque del Banco en los años noventa: una mayor relevancia

La relevancia de la asistencia del Banco aumentó notablemente durante la crisis macroeconómica de 1990-91 y en el período inmediatamente posterior. Durante la primera mitad el decenio de 1990, el Banco se centró en algunas áreas cruciales de la reforma para el crecimiento sostenible (mejor gestión macroeconómica y liberalización de los regímenes de comercio e inversión) y en el desarrollo humano (mejora de amplia base en los servicios sociales primarios). Amplió también su apoyo a la protección ambiental y dedicó más atención a mejorar la participación. Cuando los resultados en términos de desarrollo fueron poco satisfactorios, el Banco redujo los préstamos (a prácticamente cero en el sector de la energía) y emprendió amplios estudios sectoriales.

En la segunda mitad el decenio de 1990 y muy particularmente después de 1997, la relevancia de la asistencia del Banco para la reducción de la pobreza mejoró. A mediados de los años noventa, el Banco comenzó a centrar la asistencia en la reforma de los estados, con considerables logros. Pero habría sido conveniente una mayor insistencia en la gestión fiscal, la reforma del sector público y del poder judicial, la política agrícola y el desarrollo rural y la igualdad entre el hombre y la mujer.

En términos generales, las metas estratégicas del Banco durante ese decenio fueron relevantes, y mejoró el diseño de la estrategia de asistencia. La eficacia se califica como modesta, sobre todo por la limitada

FRANÇAIS

l'est. Au cours de la deuxième moitié des années 1990, quelques états ont lancé d'importantes réformes concernant leurs politiques et leurs institutions; néanmoins, encore aujourd'hui, c'est un vaste programme de réformes que l'Inde doit entreprendre au niveau des états et du gouvernement fédéral.

La Stratégie de la Banque dans les Années 1990 : Un Programme Plus Pertinent

L'aide de la Banque est devenue beaucoup plus pertinente pendant et juste après la crise macroéconomique de 1990-91. Pendant la première moitié des années 1990, la Banque a concentré son attention sur des réformes vitales pour une croissance durable (une meilleure gestion macroéconomique et la libéralisation de la réglementation du commerce et des investissements) et pour le développement humain (un vaste programme d'amélioration des services sociaux de base). Elle a également ment accru son aide à la protection de l'environnement et s'est intéressée davantage à l'amélioration des processus participatifs. Là où les résultats obtenus n'étaient pas satisfaisants, la Banque réduisait ses prêts (à pratiquement zéro dans le secteur de l'énergie) et lançait de grands programmes d'études sectorielles.

Pendant la deuxième moitié des années 1990 et surtout depuis 1997, la Banque a amélioré la nature de ses interventions pour la réduction de la pauvreté. Vers le milieu des années 1990, la Banque a commencé à s'intéresser, avec succès, aux états réformateurs. Mais il aurait été souhaitable d'accorder une plus haute priorité à la gestion budgétaire,

ENGLISH

poverty reduction has been sharpened, a more selective approach to state assistance has been put in place, and greater attention is being given to governance and institutions, although it is still too early to judge the efficacy of these initiatives.

Next Steps

India has built strong foundations for development. The Bank's main challenge is to support far-reaching reforms, at both the state and central government levels, with high-quality and widely disseminated policy studies and policy-based sector and program loans. The five pillars of the 1997 CAS remain valid:

- Support policy reform in key areas, including rural development, power, urban management, and urban water supply and sanitation.
- Focus on poverty alleviation, including a large and expanding social lending program and new initiatives for community participation and demand-driven small investments in the poorest districts.
- Increase the priority of social and environmental impacts of Bank operations.
- Promote private sector development, including the financial sector.
- Concentrate assistance on states and programs strongly committed to reform.

The fiscal and structural reform triggers for lending embodied in the CAS remain appropriate as well. Only adjustments to accelerate and assure the full application of the pillars and triggers appear necessary.

ESPAÑOL

contribución del Banco a las reformas fiscales y estructurales, la inexistencia de una estrategia eficaz de asistencia para la reducción de la pobreza rural y por la mediocre calidad de los proyectos en el momento de su conclusión. Los efectos del desarrollo institucional han sido también modestos, y la sostenibilidad incierta, dados los graves desequilibrios fiscales subsistentes, los altos costos ambientales y los problemas de gobierno. En conjunto, estas calificaciones permiten considerar que el resultado global de la asistencia durante el decenio ha sido moderadamente satisfactorio.

Al considerar estas calificaciones, hay que tener también en cuenta que desde hace poco la estrategia de asistencia resulta mucho más relevante, sobre todo por las innovaciones plasmadas en la estrategia de asistencia al país de 1997. Se ha conseguido una mayor atención a la reducción de la pobreza, un planteamiento más selectivo de la asistencia a los estados y un mayor interés en el sistema de gobierno y las instituciones, aunque es todavía demasiado pronto para juzgar la eficacia de estas iniciativas.

Próximas medidas

La India ha construido sólidos cimientos para el desarrollo. El principal desafío del Banco es apoyar reformas de largo alcance, tanto en los estados como en el gobierno central, con estudios sobre políticas de alta calidad y ampliamente difundidos acompañados de préstamos para programas y sectores orientados a la reforma de las políticas. Los cinco pilares de la estrategia de asistencia de 1997 continúan siendo válidos:

FRANÇAIS

à la réforme du secteur public et du pouvoir judiciaire, à la politique agricole, au développement rural et à l'égalité des sexes.

Dans l'ensemble, les objectifs de la Banque au cours de cette période étaient sains et la structure de sa stratégie d'assistance est meilleur. Les notes données sur le plan de l'efficacité restent modestes, surtout à cause du faible impact de la Banque sur la réforme budgétaire et d'autres réformes structurelles, de son incapacité de mettre au point une stratégie efficace de réduction de la pauvreté rurale et de la qualité médiocre de certains projets achevés. La Banque n'a eu qu'une influence modeste sur le développement institutionnel et la durabilité de ses interventions est incertaine en raison de la persistance de graves déficits budgétaires, de sérieux problèmes d'environnement et de la faiblesse de la gouvernance. La synthèse de toutes ces notes permet de conclure que, dans l'ensemble, les résultats obtenus pendantt dix ans d'assistance ont été modérément satisfaisants.

Néanmoins, cette appréciation doit être corrigée pour tenir compte d'une nette amélioration de la stratégie d'assistance au cours des dernières années, grâce surtout aux innovations introduites dans le document de stratégie de 1997. Une plus haute priorité est maintenant accordée à la réduction de la pauvreté, l'aide aux états est devenue plus sélective et une attention plus grande est apportée à la gouvernance et au développement des institutions; cependant, il est encore trop tôt pour juger de l'efficacité de ces initiatives.

ENGLISH

Recommendations

Lending Link. The Bank should link the overall lending volumes to fiscal discipline at the federal level and to progress in structural reforms in agriculture and the implementation of an effective rural development strategy. Progress in these areas is essential to poverty reduction. The current link between overall lending volume and fiscal discipline and between sectoral lending volumes and sector-specific policy and institutional frameworks would be maintained.

New Lending. New lending should be concentrated in reforming states, where an assistance strategy has been agreed with the state government. In nonreforming states, assistance should be limited to policy dialogue, clarification of performance criteria, economic and sector work to contribute to the internal debate, and pilot projects that demonstrate the benefits of policy and institutional reform. In the same manner, sectoral lending volumes should be linked to agreements on sector-specific policies and institutional frameworks.

Monitoring. Although Bank assistance has become increasingly propoor in recent years, the Bank should systematically monitor the poverty and gender impacts of Bank-assisted projects and programs. Given the large gender gap, the Bank should also make greater efforts to mainstream gender beyond the social sectors. It should enlist government agencies to do the same for public expenditure programs.

Aid Coordination. The Bank should continue to endorse government preparation and direction of formal aid coordination meetings

ESPAÑOL

- Apoyo a la reforma de políticas en las áreas clave, en particular el desarrollo rural, la electricidad, la gestión urbana y el abastecimiento de agua y saneamiento en las ciudades.
- Atención a la reducción de la pobreza, con inclusión de un programa amplio y creciente de préstamos sociales y nuevas iniciativas para la participación de la comunidad y pequeñas inversiones impulsadas por la demanda en los distritos más pobres.
- Mayor prioridad de los efectos sociales y ambientales de las operaciones del Banco.
- Promoción del desarrollo del sector privado, incluido el sector financiero.
- Concentración de la asistencia en los estados y programas fuertemente comprometidos con la reforma.

Los requisitos de reforma fiscal y estructural, establecidos como desencadenantes para el financiamiento en la estrategia de asistencia al país, continúan siendo también válidos. Sólo parecen necesarios algunos ajustes para acelerar y garantizar la plena aplicación de los pilares y desencadenantes.

Recomendaciones

Vinculación con los préstamos. El Banco debería vincular el volumen global de los préstamos a la disciplina fiscal en el plano federal y al progreso de las reformas estructurales en la agricultura y la aplicación de una estrategia de desarrollo rural eficaz. El progreso en esas áreas es fundamental para la reducción de la pobreza. Se man-

FRANÇAIS

Prochaines Étapes

L'Inde a établi de solides fondations pour son développement futur. Le principal défi de la Banque est de soutenir de profondes réformes au niveau des états et du gouvernement fédéral, grâce à des études de haute qualité qui devront être largement disséminées et au moyen de prêts programmes et de prêts sectoriels pour la réforme des politiques. Les cinq principales composantes de la stratégie de 1997 restent valables:

- Appui aux réformes de politiques dans les secteur prioritaires, notamment le développement rural, l'énergie, l'urbanisme, les adductions d'eau et l'assainissement dans les villes.
- Concentration sur la lutte contre la pauvreté, grâce notamment à une forte expansion des prêts aux secteurs sociaux, à de nouvelles initiatives de participation des communautés et à de petits investissement dans les districts les plus pauvres, répondant à la demande des populations.
- Une plus grande priorité à l'impact social et environnemental des opérations de la Banque.
- Le développement du secteur privé, y compris du secteur financier.
- Concentration de l'aide aux états et des financements de programmes en fonction de la vigueur de l'engagement en faveur des réformes.

Les conditions définies par le document de stratégie en ce qui concerne la réforme budgétaire et les réformes structurelles restent également valables. Quelques ajustements paraissent nécessaires pour accélérer et renforcer l'exécution des principaux objectifs et conditions.

ENGLISH

and to provide logistical support. To enhance the effectiveness of external assistance and partnerships, and to enable greater selectivity, the Bank should strengthen informal, in-country donor coordination of country assistance strategies and critical sector strategies, such as agriculture and rural development.

ESPAÑOL

tendría la habitual conexión entre el volumen global de los préstamos y la disciplina fiscal y entre el volumen de los préstamos sectoriales y las políticas relativas a sectores específicos y los marcos institucionales.

Nuevo financiamiento. El nuevo financiamiento debería concentrarse en los estados interesados en la reforma, cuando se haya acordado una estrategia de asistencia con el gobierno estatal. En los estados no partidarios de la reforma la asistencia debería limitarse al diálogo sobre políticas, la aclaración de los criterios de desempeño, los estudios económicos y sectoriales para contribuir al debate interno y proyectos piloto que demuestren los beneficios de la reforma normativa e institucional. De la misma manera, el volumen de los préstamos sectoriales debería vincularse a acuerdos sobre marcos institucionales y políticas relacionados con sectores específicos.

Seguimiento. Aunque en los últimos años la asistencia del Banco se ha centrado cada vez más en los pobres, el Banco debería supervisar sistemáticamente los efectos de los proyectos y programas respaldados por él en la lucha contra la pobreza y el logro de una mayor igualdad entre el hombre y la mujer. Dadas las enormes diferencias en este terreno, el Banco debería también hacer mayor esfuerzo por incorporar este tema en las actividades habituales, más allá de los sectores sociales. Debería conseguir también que los organismos gubernamentales hicieran otro tanto con los programas de gasto público.

Coordinación de la ayuda. El Banco debería continuar respaldando la preparación y dirección

FRANÇAIS

Recommandations

Conditions des Prêts. La Banque doit lier le volume global de ses prêts à la discipline budgétaire au niveau fédéral, aux progrès des réformes structurelles dans l'agriculture et à la mise en œuvre d'une stratégie efficace de développement rural. Des progrès dans ces domaines sont essentiels pour réduire la pauvreté. Les conditions présentes qui lient le volume global des prêts à la discipline budgétaire et le volume des prêts sectoriels aux réformes des politiques et des institutions sectorielles doivent être maintenues.

Prêts Nouveaux. Les nouveaux prêts doivent être concentrés dans les états réformateurs sur la base d'un accord sur la stratégie d'assistance avec le gouvernement de chaque état. Dans les états qui refusent les réformes, l'aide doit être limitée au dialogue de politiques, à la clarification des critères de performance, aux études économiques et sectorielles permettant de faciliter les débats internes et à des projets pilotes visant à démontrer les avantages de la réforme des politiques et des institutions. De la même façon, le volume des prêts sectoriels doit être lié à des accords précis sur les politiques et le cadre institutionnel.

Suivi. Au cours des dernières années, la Banque s'est de plus en plus intéressée à la lutte contre la pauvreté; la Banque doit aussi organiser un suivi systématique de l'impact de ses projets et programmes sur la pauvreté et la condition féminine. Compte tenu de la gravité de l'inégalité entre les sexes, la Banque doit intensifier ses efforts pour intégrer ce facteur dans l'ensemble de ses opérations au delà

ESPAÑOL

gubernamental de las reuniones formales de coordinación de ayuda y ofreciendo apoyo logístico. Para aumentar la eficacia de la asistencia externa y de las asociaciones y hacer posible una mayor selectividad, el Banco debería reforzar la coordinación informal de los donantes dentro del país en lo que se refiere a las estrategias de asistencia de alcance nacional y las relativas a sectores críticos, como la agricultura y el desarrollo rural.

FRANÇAIS

des seuls secteurs sociaux. Elle doit également mobiliser l'appui des agences gouvernementales pour que les mêmespratiques soient étendues aux programmes de dépenses publiques.

Coordination de l'Aide. La Banque doit continuer de soutenir les efforts du gouvernement pour la préparation et la coordination des réunions officielles de coordination de l'aide; cet appui doit être accompagné d'un soutien logistique. Pour accroître l'efficacité de l'aide extérieure et des partenariats et pour favoriser la sélectivité, la Banque doit renforcer les réunions informelles des bailleurs de fonds dans le pays pour la coordination des stratégies d'assistance, globalement et pour les secteurs les plus importants, tels que l'agriculture et le développement rural.

ABBREVIATIONS AND ACRONYMS

AIDS	Acquired Immunodeficiency Syndrome
CAE	Country Assistance Evaluation
CARE	Cooperative for Assistance and Relief Everywhere
CAS	Country Assistance Strategy
CEM	Country Economic Memoranda
CODE	Committee on Development Effectiveness
DEC	Development Economics & Chief Economist
DFID	Department for International Development
DPEPs	District Primary Education projects
EAP	East Asia and Pacific Region
ESW	Economic and sector work
GDP	Gross domestic product
GoI	Government of India
HIV	Human Immunodeficiency Virus
IBRD	International Bank for Reconstruction and Development
ICICI	Industrial Credit and Investment Corporation of India
IDA	International Development Association
IFC	International Finance Corporation
M&E	Monitoring and evaluation
NGO	Nongovernmental organization
NTPC	National Thermal Power Corporation
OED	Operations Evaluation Department
OEDST	Operations Evaluation Department Sector and Thematic Evaluation
PER	Public Expenditure Review
PIU	Project Implementation Unit
PREM	Poverty Reduction and Economic Management Network
QAG	Quality Assurance Group
SAC	Structural Adjustment Credit
SAL	Structural Adjustment Loan
SC	Informal Subcommittee of the Committee on Development Effectiveness
SDC	Swiss Agency for Development Cooperation
UNDP	United Nations Development Programme
UPBEP	Uttar Pradesh Basic Education Project
VEC	Village Education Committee
WTO	World Trade Organization

INDIA'S DEVELOPMENT RECORD

From Independence through the 1980s

Indian civilization is deeply rooted and far reaching. Long before the end of the first millennium, India had made seminal contributions to mathematics, astronomy, architecture, metallurgy, medicine, weaving, dyeing, fine arts, language, and philosophy. Tolerance and spirituality characterize the country's rich culture.[1] When the British began establishing colonial rule in the 18th century, India's economy was strong in trade, commercial agriculture, and labor-intensive industry, especially textiles. Its political structure, however, was fragmented and its income distribution highly unequal. At independence in 1947, India had made remarkable strides in political consolidation and the rise of an educated elite, but it remained an acutely impoverished nation burdened by a surging population.

Eradicating poverty became the declared overarching objective of India's development strategy. A broad national consensus soon emerged on the means to achieve this objective—rapid growth through industrialization and redistributive transfers to the poor. India's development policies welded two disparate visions: Mahatma Gandhi's dream of a simple, village-based economy and Nehru's socialist ideal of a self-reliant welfare state. In deference to both, the government subsidized small-scale industries and handicrafts and intervened extensively in the economy through publicly owned heavy industries and direct controls. Economic openness was viewed with suspicion. A series of five-year plans gave concrete shape to this strategy in line with the development paradigm of the time.[2]

Government control over the economy and the large role of public investment in productive activities generated some social benefits but also had a significant negative side. The industrial licensing system, the restrictions on capital flows, and the complex system of high trade barriers reduced competition, thwarted enterprise restructuring, generated monopoly rents, and stifled growth. Paradoxically, the public sector—with its human and financial resources overstretched—lacked the capacity to intervene effectively on behalf of the poor; that is, by providing universal schooling and basic medical facilities.

The proportion of poor people fluctuated around 50 percent through the 1970s (see figure 1.1), when the average per capita income growth rate was below 1 percent.[3] The higher per capita growth of the 1980s, estimated at 3.5 percent, reduced poverty to around 34 percent. But the high growth was unsustainable as it relied on excessive public spending and financing of the fiscal deficit at commercial rates. Moreover, the unintended bias against labor intensity was such that output growth in the industrial sector during 1951–91 did not contribute to poverty reduction at all, either in urban or rural areas. Instead, poverty reduction was positively affected by growth in the agricultural and service sectors, and by human capital development (Ravallion and Datt 1996).

By the 1980s India had eradicated famine and attained self-sufficiency in food production. The Bank played a modest role in helping create the physical and institutional infrastructure of the Green Revolution, but the Bank's role in sustaining the revolution was critical (Lele and Bumb 1995). India also made significant gains in social indicators, with some southern states (led by Kerala) succeeding in bringing fertility

to replacement levels. Between 1970 and the late 1980s life expectancy rose from 49 to 60 years, infant mortality fell from 137 to 80 per thousand, and the annual population growth rate fell from 2.3 percent to 2 percent. Primary enrollment rose from 73 percent to 97 percent.

But social indicators trailed behind those of China and many other low-income countries. By the end of the 1980s, with only modest steps toward economic reform, India also trailed in the global economic competition, the result of "closure to trade and investment; a license-obsessed, restrictive state; inability to sustain social expenditures; loss of confidence in the efficacy of growth in reducing poverty; macro instability, indeed crisis; pessimism; and marginalization of India in world affairs" (Bhagwati 1998).

The 1990s: Far-Reaching Reform[4]

The Gulf War's temporary effect of raising oil prices and disrupting remittance inflows highlighted India's macroeconomic weakness. By June 1991, with reserves exhausted, India faced serious external debt service problems. Per capita economic growth turned negative. The macro-

Figure 1.1 Poverty, Inequality, and Consumption per Capita, 1971–97

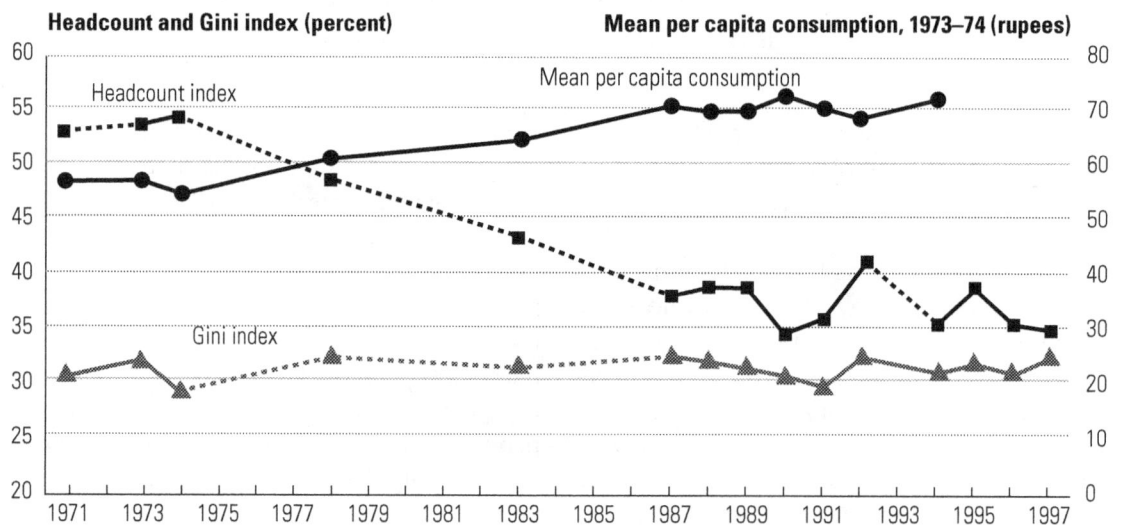

Note: Data points for headcount and Gini indexes for 1995–97 are estimates. Missing data points are connected with a dotted line.
Source: Datt 1997.

economic crisis, the break up of the Soviet Union and its economic development model, and the example of reforming China's economic success created the opportunity for the reformers to take over policymaking. Understanding the need to go beyond stabilization measures, a new government introduced two major structural policy changes. It dismantled industrial licensing, except for 18 industries, and initiated the liberalization of foreign trade and exchange.

The new approach aimed at giving the private sector a greater role in India's development by improving the investment and tax regimes, reorienting foreign investment policy, opening infrastructure to private investment, reforming public enterprises and the financial sector, and reducing price controls. The government also expanded its poverty alleviation programs.

These reforms yielded positive results. Per capita income rebounded to $390 by 1998 after dropping from its 1990 peak of $360. Export growth was brisk until 1996, after which it slowed but did not stop. Annual per capita output growth increased to 3 percent in 1992–94, reached 5 percent in 1994–96, and has remained around 3–4 percent since. Through the financial turmoil in East Asia, inflation rates stayed moderate, the balance of payments stayed healthy, and external reserves increased. Thus the first stage of market liberalization has been a macroeconomic success. Moreover, the economy became more integrated with the global economy and experienced a large increase of private investment.

In the mid-1990s frequent government changes and associated electoral cycles slowed the pace of reform. And the past three years have seen backsliding in trade liberalization (a 4.5 percent import surcharge in 1998) and fiscal management. Subsidies remain large. Expenditure composition in both the center and the states is deteriorating toward salaries, pensions, and interest payments. Revenues are falling. After bottoming out around a still high 8 percent of GDP in 1994–97, the consolidated public deficit rose to above 11 percent in 1999–2000, exactly the same as at the start of the decade. This again raised the risk of macroeconomic instability, crowding out credit to the private sector and public development spending because of the high interest cost of the large and rising stock of government debt (see table 1.1). In public enterprise reform, India has so far preferred slow "disinvestment" of minority stakes to privatizing viable units or closing unviable ones. Much "learning by doing" regarding the regulatory framework for private sector participation was combined with inadequate public investment in infrastructure, a major bottleneck (Ahluwalia 1999). Finally, labor market rigidities remained untouched.

India is still a low-income country with high poverty, ill health, malnutrition, illiteracy, a large gender gap, and deep social divisions (see table 1.2). Caste still matters: while two-thirds of all Indian women and two-fifths of all Indian men are illiterate, 81 percent of all scheduled caste women and 54 percent of all scheduled caste men are illiterate. India ranks 132 out of 174 countries in the Human Development Index (UNDP 1999). Moreover, environmental damage (unsafe water supplies and sanitation, soil degradation, and air pollution) estimated in the range of 4.5 to 8 percent of GDP a year offsets much of the gain from economic growth (Brandon and Hommann 1995, Khanna and Babu 1997, Tata Energy Research Institute 1998).[5]

The states differ substantially in poverty levels and trends. Poverty has increased in Bihar, Madhya Pradesh, Orissa, Rajasthan, and Uttar Pradesh, where the bulk of the poor live. It has declined in Andhra Pradesh, Gujarat, Kerala, Maharashtra, and Punjab. The highest rate of decline occurred in Kerala (both rural and urban poverty incidence have been halved since the 1970s), which among the states has the highest proportion of villages with electricity, a high road density, a high proportion of land under irrigation, and by far the highest female literacy rate. The earlier investment in education and rural development enabled Keralites to take advantage of the opportunities that opened up in the Gulf from the mid-1970s and to use the resulting inflow of remittances effectively.

According to World Bank estimates of poverty based on official expenditure surveys and price indexes, aggregate progress in poverty reduction has been disappointing. Poverty incidence worsened to 41 percent in 1992 because of negative per capita income growth and higher food prices (due to poor harvests and limited imports). In the following years growth picked up and poverty

Table 1.1	Selected Economic Indicators										
Indicator	**1989**	**1990**	**1991**	**1992**	**1993**	**1994**	**1995**	**1996**	**1997**	**1998**	**1999**
Annual GDP growth (percent)	6.6	5.7	0.4	5.4	5.0	7.9	8.0	7.3	5.0	6.1	6.1
Annual GNP per capita growth (percent)	4.4	3.5	−1.8	3.5	3.1	6.1	6.4	5.7	3.3	4.2	4.4
Gross domestic fixed investment (percent of GDP)	21.8	22.5	21.5	21.8	20.9	21.4	23.8	23.2	22.9	22.7	23.1
Public sector (percent of GDP)	9.0	8.8	9.0	8.0	7.8	8.6	7.5	6.6	6.8	6.6	6.3
Private sector (percent of GDP)	11.9	12.7	11.7	12.9	13.1	12.9	16.3	16.6	16.1	16.2	16.8
Inflation (CPI, annual percent)	6.2	11.6	13.5	9.6	7.5	8.1	12.2	9.3	7.0	13.1	6.4
Real effective exchange rate (1990 = 100)	111.1	100.0	85.4	72.0	71.5	74.2	72.0	70.4	76.3	73.6	72.5
Overall public sector deficit	−11.6	−11.3	−9.5	−9.2	−10.1	−9.1	−8.2	−8.7	−8.5	−9.7	−11.2
Public sector debt	..	85.5	88.7	89.9	88.7	83.7	79.1	75.7	77.4	76.6	80.9
Current account balance (percent of GDP)	−1.8	−2.5	−0.2	−1.2	−0.3	−1.1	−1.8	−1.4	−1.3	−1.0	−1.4
Exports, annual growth (percent)	13.7	9.1	10.8	6.9	14.4	8.0	32.9	7.1	6.2	4.4	8.1
Imports, annual growth (percent)	−0.6	3.2	−12.0	18.6	11.1	17.5	20.5	10.1	11.7	5.6	5.5
External debt (percent of GNP)	25.7	26.3	31.9	34.8	34.2	31.4	26.2	23.7	22.6	23.0	22.1
Debt service (percent of exports)	28.6	32.7	29.2	28.1	25.4	25.8	27.4	22.2	18.6	17.0	16.8
Foreign exchange reserves (months of imports)	1.9	1.0	4.0	4.0	6.6	6.6	4.6	5.4	5.7	6.1	6.0

Source: World Bank Unified Survey 2000, IMF staff estimates (for fiscal estimates).

Table 1.2	Key Social Indicators, 1980–98											
	India			**China**			**Sub-Saharan Africa**			**Low-income**		
Indicator	**1980**	**1990**	**95–98**	**1980**	**1990**	**95–98**	**1980**	**1990**	**95–98**	**1990**	**1990**	**95–98**
Illiteracy rate, adult total (percent of people 15+)	56.4	47.8	43.5	34.0	22.2	16.5	61.1	49.8	39.4	46.8	36.9	38.5
Female (percent of females 15+)	70.2	60.7	n.a.	47.3	31.9	25.5	71.4	59.1	49.6	60.0	47.9	42.0
Male (percent of males 15+)	43.6	35.9	32.2	21.4	13.0	8.8	50.4	40.3	31.1	34.2	26.2	29.1
Gross primary school enrollment (percent)	80.0	100.1	89.7	113.0	125.0	118.0	78.0	75.7	..	94.0	102.5	104.3
Female (percent)	64.1	85.5	81.2	104.0	120.0	117.0	66.5	67.8	..	82.7	94.0	98.4
Male (percent)	95.5	113.9	97.5	121.0	130.0	118.0	87.0	82.7	..	104.6	110.8	108.7
Gross secondary school enrollment (percent)	30.0	44.0	49.0	46.0	49.0	67.0	15.0	23.4	..	33.6	40.1	53.7
Female (percent)	20.0	33.0	38.0	37.0	42.0	63.0	10.0	21.0	..	25.5	32.9	47.2
Male (percent)	39.0	55.5	62.4	54.0	56.0	70.0	19.7	26.2	..	41.2	47.4	59.3
Life expectancy at birth, total (years)	50.4	52.8	63.1	66.9	68.9	69.9	47.6	50.1	50.4	58.2	61.4	59.7
Infant mortality rate (per 1,000 live births)	110.0	80.0	69.8	42.0	33.1	31.1	114.8	100.2	91.8	97.5	74.7	77.4

n.a. Not available.
a. Latest enrollment data are for 1995.
Source: Department of Economic Affairs, Ministry of Finance, India (except for secondary school enrollment) and SIMA database, World Bank.

declined in both rural (to 36 percent) and urban (to 30 percent) areas by 1997, but at a slower pace than India had experienced in the 1980s. Yet, rural poverty was higher in 1997 than at the beginning of the decade (see figure 1.1). But a contrasting hypothesis of faster urban and rural poverty reduction during the 1990s has recently been proposed on the basis of the rising private consumption growth estimates recorded in the national accounts (Bhalla 2000) and of alternative price estimates for the deflator of rural household consumption (Deaton and Tarozzi 1999).

Controversies about poverty numbers are not new to India and are quickly seized upon by opponents and proponents of reform. Regardless of which numbers are right, India has never been a good performer in poverty reduction by the standards of East Asia (Ravallion 2000). Growth has actually slowed in the poorer states. Moreover, comparing a near 50 percent reduction in the growth rate of real agricultural wages in the 1990s to the the rate in the previous decade suggests that the poverty-reducing impact of agricultural growth has declined. Among the possible explanations are slower labor demand associated with new crops, a slowdown in agricultural productivity growth, and a slowdown of agricultural growth in the eastern states, where poverty is concentrated. Finally, there was sluggish employment creation in the nonfarm rural economy (World Bank 2000).

For India as a whole, inequality measured by the Gini coefficient has declined slowly but steadily by about 0.3 percent a year since the early 1950s, with some leveling in the 1990s to around 34 percent. Inequality remains higher in urban (36.5 percent) than in rural areas (30.4 percent; Datt 1999). But the weaker effects of growth on poverty observed in the 1990s may stem in part from rising inequality that the surveys may not fully capture. An illiterate Indian woman, a member of the scheduled tribe or caste, and a landless wage earner face significantly higher-than-average risks of poverty.

Strong Foundations for Development

Based on policies prevailing in the mid-1990s, predictions of some researchers using cross-country growth regressions revealed a per capita growth rate of 3.6 percent a year beyond 1996, only slightly less than actual. Their simulations showed that India could have doubled its per capita growth rate if it had adopted East Asian policies on public savings, openness, labor market flexibility, and government spending (Bajpai and Sachs 1997). While these estimates are only indicative, they suggest that India could grow at a rate higher than the 4 percent recorded in the past four years if it resumed the faster pace of reform of the early 1990s.

Beyond growth and macroeconomic stability, researchers and policy analysts have reached a broad consensus on the factors affecting the pace of poverty reduction in India: more effective public development spending to enhance infrastructure (especially in rural areas), human capital, and agricultural productivity (Datt and Ravallion 1998; Ravallion and Datt 1999). In turn, policy, institutional, and governance frameworks influence the accumulation of physical and human capital, their efficient allocation, and technological innovation and adoption (Srinivasan 2001).

Widespread agreement has also emerged across the political spectrum on the need to rejuvenate the reform process. This view—articulated in the past five years in economic journals, policy studies, government committee deliberations, and Bank reports—has been endorsed by all past coalition governments and reaffirmed strongly by the current one. But the belief that a second round of reform would entail high political risks is still widespread. Though the bureaucracy's mindset has already begun to change, resistance to reform comes also from vested interests that gain from the complex incentive structure. Preoccupation with issues of ethnicity and religion, regional pulls and pressures, and the ideological baggage of economic nationalism remain obstacles to sustained reform.

A Large, Unfinished Reform Agenda

Business surveys and qualitative assessments of India's economic management and institutional performance in the 1990s confirm that there have been substantial improvements in many areas, but they also point to remaining deficiencies in public sector management, regulatory frameworks, labor market policies, corporate governance and exit policy, banking sector efficiency, and trade protection.[6] High corporate tax rates (35 percent for domestic companies and 48 percent for foreign companies), in particular, are a disincentive to private investment.

Fiscal Reform

Reducing the fiscal deficit should be a priority, but little progress on this front is expected this year (2000–01). The public bureaucracy needs streamlining. Public programs for marketing food and other commodities (including the still ineffective Public Distribution System) need further reform, as do programs for employment and training. Subsidies (about 14.4 percent of GDP) and public enterprise losses need to be reduced. Expenditures need to be redirected toward operations and maintenance and investment in infrastructure.[7] To improve revenue buoyancy and equity, the tax base needs broadening and tax administration needs improvement.

Governance

Variable enforcement of laws, regulations, and contracts and delayed administration of justice are serious problems, especially with respect to the poor. The chain of accountability from the civil service to the legislature is weak.[8] Oversight and audit reports have limited impact because of a lack of transparency, delays, and poor follow-up by parliamentary oversight committees. State administrative and financial control capacities have large gaps and variations. The performance of the civil service is undermined by overstaffing, low salaries, inadequate performance appraisals, and political interference. Corruption, which extends to the police and judicial systems, is perceived to be serious.

Much work lies ahead to improve weak governance. In addition to strengthening financial accountability, public sector reforms require focus on quality, efficiency, incentives for service delivery, and orientation toward a market economy. The legal system also needs strengthening to fight corruption and uphold equality under the law. Devolution of power has been gradual since the landmark 1992 constitutional amendment mandated decentralization of state responsibilities to elected local bodies, or *panchayats,* and enhanced representation of women in such bodies.

Training is needed to improve local capacity for administration and service delivery.

Private and Financial Sector Development

A major constraint to private sector development is slow privatization of public enterprises, including banks, due in part to a blurred delineation of responsibilities among the multiple government agencies and commissions that advise on and implement privatization.[9] Overly protective labor laws need to be relaxed; archaic bankruptcy and liquidation laws and procedures (including the Sick Industrial Company Act) urgently need reform. Completing the enabling legislation and regulatory institutions will allow an expansion of private sector participation in infrastructure. The regulatory framework for corporate governance also needs more transparency.

Openness

Protection remains very high compared with all large countries in Asia and Latin America (the effective rate of protection on the secondary sector was 47.6 percent in 1998) and, thus, the liberalization timetable to correct the still substantial anti-export bias of the current regime should be accelerated. Even internally, India is not a single common market, especially in agriculture—interstate sales taxes and movement restrictions across and within states still apply.

Agricultural Reform

Agriculture remains overregulated, with distorted production and marketing incentives. Public resources are used inefficiently, mostly for public employees' salaries and subsidies for water, electricity, fertilizer, and food that do not reach the poorest. Basic reforms are needed to free internal trade, eliminate other market distortions, and integrate India fully with world markets while increasing investment in agricultural technology and rural infrastructure, protecting the poor, and ensuring that quality inputs are supplied.[10]

Environmental Protection

Environmental legislation is adequate, but current efforts to strengthen the weak enforcement capacity must be accompanied by policy changes. To stem over-watering and excessive private pumping from aquifers, subsidies for electricity and water should be drastically reduced. Community-based programs hold promise for improved natural resource management, but scaling them up requires increased public funding. A more effective public role for urban sanitation services is also needed.

Social Sectors

Public education can be effective, as in Madhya Pradesh, where local communities successfully took responsibility for hiring teachers and monitoring their performance. At the same time, national enrollment levels in primary schools remain lower than in comparator countries. Improving service delivery of health and education services for better efficiency and access by the poor requires increasing public expenditures, reallocating expenditures away from tertiary levels and toward primary ones, making institutional changes, and sharpening targeting and incentives.

Social Inclusion

India's public sector has an affirmative action program, which applies to elected bodies, to help break caste inequality. Reservation of a third of local council seats for women, decreed by the 1992 Panchayats Act, is already raising the voice of poor women in local politics. India's gender strategy aims to empower women socially and economically by changing attitudes toward girls; providing education, training, employment, and support services; and emphasizing women's rights and laws. This strategy should be pursued with renewed vigor, sensitively mainstreaming exclusion concerns in all development programs and monitoring their gender-disaggregated and caste-disaggregated impact.

2

THE INDIA–WORLD BANK HISTORICAL RELATIONSHIP

External Development Assistance and the Bank's Contribution

External financing has always been a substantial fraction of India's public investment: long-term public borrowing from abroad has ranged from 1.7 percent of GDP (in the 1980s) to 2.5 percent (at its peak during 1992–94). Since 1995 it has been around 1.9 percent. The composition of these capital inflows has changed from an equal contribution of official and private sources in the 1980s to 52 percent private financing in 1998–2000.

India was one of the Bank's founding members, is still one of the Bank's main borrowers, and has had a major influence on the Bank's understanding of development. The Bank has been India's largest source of external capital, providing almost a third of all long-term gross inflows in the 1980s and, by the end of the 1990s, still supplying more than a fifth. Bank disbursements, which were about 5.5 percent of gross domestic public investment during the 1980s, rose to about 8 percent in the early 1990s and have been 6.2 percent since 1998. Cumulative lending from 1950 until June 2000 has been $53.8 billion for 412 projects, split equally between the International Development Association (IDA) and the International Bank for Reconstruction and Development (IBRD). Bank commitments to India have averaged about $1.6 billion annually during fiscal 1997–2000, with 54 percent from IDA and 46 percent from the IBRD. Without sanctions and with satisfactory country policy performance, however, IBRD lending in recent years would have been substantially higher (see last section of this chapter) and the blend would have been harder.

Through the 1970s: A Cyclical Relationship

The Bank's relationship with India began with a slow acquaintanceship; praise from the Bank for India's first five-year plan; cautious lending for railways, iron and steel, irrigation, and development finance; and mild criticism of the overly ambitious second five-year plan in the late 1950s.[1] Initially, the Bank and other donors supported the third five-year plan, consisting of ambitious investment programs supported by generous capital transfers. But a high-level Bank economic mission led by B. Bell criticized the government's development strategy and recommended greater liberalization, increased foreign assistance, and a currency devaluation.

Box 2.1 **Strong Local Institutions and the Right Incentives: Operation Flood**

During the 1970s and 1980s the Bank contributed $425 million to support the continued development of a cooperative system, Operation Flood, that had already assured small-scale producers a market for their milk. This led to large increases in milk production, training for villagers in dairy technology, manufacture of dairy equipment, stimulation of private sector investment, and major benefits for women. The difficulties of protecting the system from import competition, high state subsidies, and political interference in management of the cooperatives led the Bank to withdraw its support. An OED study concluded that the project provided solid and sustainable net benefits to the poor. The main lesson identified in the study was that development effectiveness of external assistance can be increased substantially by relying on sound local institutions with the right incentives.

The sense of vulnerability prevailing in India at the time, partly due to the country's increasing dependence on aid, exacerbated sensitivities about outside interference. The policy dialogue triggered by the Bell report and directed by the Bank's president became confrontational. The Bank and India became estranged, with the notable exception of agriculture (that part of the Bell report was prepared under the direction of John Crawford). For the Bank, the policy dialogue represents an early attempt to use the leverage of its lending in a major member country. While the government accepted the need for reform, Bank pressure caused resentment. The modest amount of the devaluation, combined with tariff surcharges on traditional exports, a severe drought, and inadequate relaxation of the underlying control regime proved insufficient to generate a strong supply response. Given the high political cost of the devaluation and its apparent ineffectiveness, vastly compounded by delays and shortfalls in promised quick-disbursing aid, controls were tightened again and the government emerged from this episode wary of liberalization and determined to lessen the country's dependence on foreign assistance. In parallel, the Bank's activist attitude gave way to an exaggerated reticence to advocate policy change. Instead, the Bank focused on narrow issues directly related to its operations' success, even in its quick-disbursing program lending—for example, the annual industrial imports credits.

In the late 1960s and 1970s, trust was restored. India's agricultural sector became the focus of Bank assistance, which helped expedite the adoption and dissemination of the new technologies that produced the Green Revolution. At the same time, Indian authorities—who feared Bank interference in politically sensitive national programs—resisted the Bank's ambitions to support the government's antipoverty programs. Policy advice and economic analyses, mostly produced by resident mission staff in close consultation with government officials, had a modest impact. Conditionality was used sparingly and common ground between the Bank's objectives and the government's was continually stressed.

External political factors helped cement the relationship. While assistance from the U.S. government declined, reflecting a deteriorating political relationship, Bank lending increased and soon exceeded aid flows from other donors, eliciting much goodwill from Indian officials. By the end of the 1970s India and the Bank were converging: the Bank had adopted the essence of India's outlook on developmental priorities, while India had started to cut its tangle of red tape.

The 1980s: Lending Push in a Poor Policy Environment

Throughout the 1980s most academics, government officials, and top political leaders became aware of the need to adopt a new model of economic management, but the necessary political support for far-reaching reform was not forthcoming. Bank staff produced a large number of sector reports, especially in industry and finance, that pointed to policy deficiencies that required attention.

But while the Bank was actively promoting structural adjustment in many of its member countries, high-level discussion of necessary policy adjustments in India—to say nothing of an explicit link between the Bank's lending and policy reform—was largely avoided. Throughout the 1980s, Bank management did not address India's disappointing policy record for fear of jeopardizing a strong lending relationship with a sensitive client. The Bank also muffled its advisory and institutional reporting roles.[2]

Although IDA lending slowed considerably throughout the 1980s, both as a proportion of the total and in absolute terms (in line with undertakings to the IDA deputies), IBRD lending and International Financial Corporation investments expanded very rapidly. Total Bank annual commitments reached a peak of $3 billion in fiscal 1989 and $18.5 billion for the decade (figure 2.1).

In many cases Bank-supported projects were inconsistent with Bank economic and sector analyses and advice. Many projects had limited policy content and supported the expansion of the state in the economy, regardless of efficiency. The Bank continued to lend to public sector enterprises that made fertilizer, steel, and cement; to unsound rural credit institutions; and to inefficient state electricity boards that did not charge for the power they produced and were behind serious state financial problems that have yet to be resolved.

The Bank also lent for the expansion of irrigation systems known for their inability to recover costs and clouded with the suspicion of corruption. The focus on irrigation came at the cost of neglect of rainfed areas in which a large proportion of the rural poor live. Bank lending for urban development met with considerable failure because it ignored the public finance and institutional development aspects of urban lending. The failure was so profound that it became the reason for the decision in the first half of the 1990s to withdraw entirely from the sector. Furthermore, despite the great needs in the social sectors, the Bank was not able to establish a dialogue or a lending program in health and education because of the government's resistance to foreign advice.

There were some bright spots, such as a loan to the Housing Development Corporation that helped establish housing finance in the country, and a successful project that provided resources

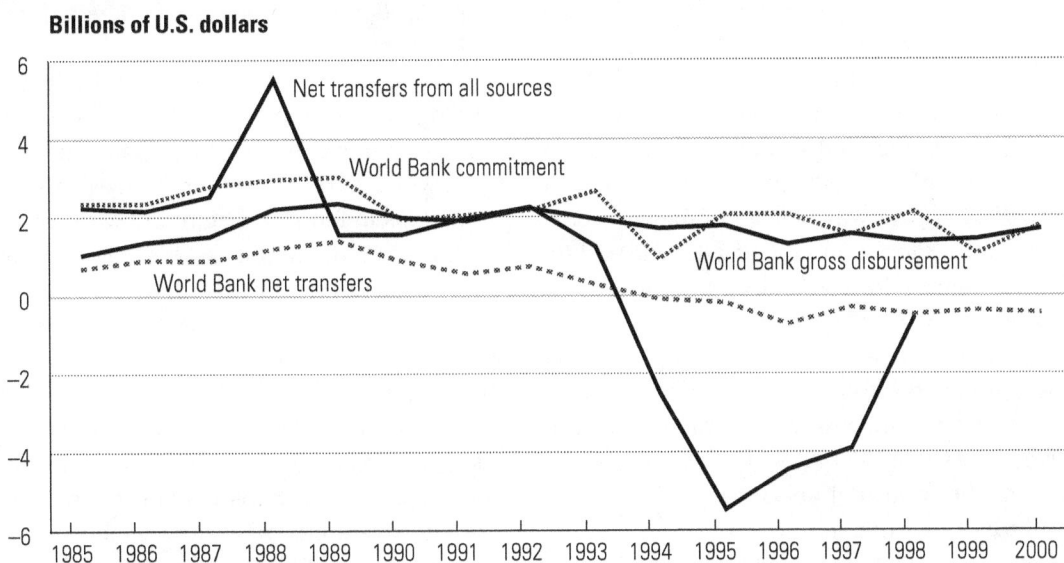

Figure 2.1   Commitments, Disbursements, and Net Transfers, 1985–2000

Source: For commitments, gross disbursements, and net transfers see Controller's database. For total net transfers see Global Development Finance database, 10 July 2000.

for venture capital and research and development. On the whole, however, in the 1980s transfer of resources was the overriding objective of the Bank, with little concern for the effectiveness with which these resources were used. As lending expanded in the wrong direction, however, the quality at entry of the Bank portfolio faltered. OED rated Bank performance at the project appraisal stage satisfactory in only 26 of 57 operations (52 percent by commitment) approved in fiscal 1985–89.

The 1990s: Enhanced Relevance of the Bank Assistance Strategy

Against the backdrop of strong commitment to structural adjustment by a new government, the relevance of Bank assistance increased markedly during and immediately after the 1990–91 macroeconomic crisis. Changing the mindset of the principal counterparts in the core ministries was not the issue any more. Instead, the central challenge was to help the newly elected, reform-minded government implement its programs, a challenge that the Bank substantially met.

Bank assistance focused on supporting macroeconomic stabilization measures (together with the International Monetary Fund); reforms in the investment and trade regimes, finance, taxation, and public enterprises; and cushioning short-term social costs, including with three quick-disbursing, policy-based operations. At the same time the Bank sought to discontinue old-style lending for public enterprises and state electricity boards, and to build a lending program in health and education. The Bank continued lending, however, in a number of sectors without a sector strategy and without seeking the necessary reforms (for example, in agriculture, irrigation, urban water supply—even banking). Nonetheless, the partial attempt to make Bank advice consistent with its lending led to a record drop in new commitments in fiscal 1994 to less than $1 billion and to the dismantling of the Industrial and Finance Division of the India Department.

For the first half of the 1990s the Bank focused on crucial areas of reforms for sustainable growth (for improved macroeconomic management and liberalization of the trade and investment regime)

and on human development (for broad-based improvement of primary social services). It also expanded its support for environmental protection. But the Bank did not pay enough attention to the inadequacy of agricultural incentives, the landless rural poor, rainfed agriculture, and the structural constraints to rural development. It also missed opportunities to reform safety nets and to improve the targeting of the poor and women in its projects and in public expenditures.

In the second half of the 1990s the relevance of Bank assistance to poverty reduction improved, and even more so after 1997. In the mid-1990s the Bank began studying state finances, increased its attention to sector reforms, offered assistance in establishing a framework conducive to efficient private investment in infrastructure, and offered its support in restructuring social programs and providing the poor with skills to participate in the new, more competitive market economy. The telecommunication companies, ports, and gas and oil sectors, which had the potential to attract private investment, were excluded from lending assistance. All new loans were expected to have a strong policy content.

The 1995 Country Assistance Strategy document (CAS) explicitly listed continued reduction of the central government's deficit to 5.5 percent in 1995–96 and beyond and progress in implementing its reform agenda as triggers for providing annual lending volumes of around $2.9 billion. The strategy also proposed discontinuing lending to states whose fiscal stance was unsustainable. Significant shortfalls against those triggers were expected to lead to progressive reductions in lending, beginning with IBRD operations, to a minimum of $1.2 billion annually. But the government made clear to the Bank, as well as to the International Monetary Fund, that it preferred to follow its own pace in reforming the economy and that it did not see a role for the Bank in framing the agenda. In spite of the inadequate fiscal stance (see table 1.1), the downward adjustment in Bank lending volume did not happen, and annual new commitments returned to more than $2 billion in fiscal 1995 and 1996.

The most recent full CAS, in December 1997, contained triggers similar to those in the 1995 CAS for overall annual lending of about $3 billion. It was built around the same objective of poverty reduction through accelerated growth and social development as past assistance strategies. But it added specific antipoverty interventions. It also set out a new and highly relevant operational approach to deal with the challenge of finding a role for the Bank in supporting reforms; that is, to scale up lending to reforming states. And for the first time the CAS articulated monitorable targets against which the success of assistance can be judged. The Bank aimed to contribute by 2010 to:

- Reducing poverty to 15 percent
- Halving the proportion of malnourished children
- Putting in place a reliable disease surveillance system
- Increasing contraceptive prevalence to more than 60 percent of eligible couples
- Reducing the population growth rate to 1.2 percent (from 1.9 percent).

The five operational pillars of the 1997 strategy, still highly relevant, were:

- Support for policy reform (through early engagement and building consensus and ownership with partners and clients) in key areas, including rural development, power, urban management, and urban water supply and sanitation.

- Focus on poverty alleviation, including a large and expanding social lending program and new initiatives for community participation and demand-driven small investments in the poorest districts (see box 2.2).
- Increased priority to the social and environmental impacts of Bank operations.
- Promotion of private sector development, including the financial sector.
- Concentration of assistance toward states and programs strongly committed to reform.

Some components of the 1997 CAS have progressed well. Bank assistance has focused increasingly on rural development; social and human development; participatory, decentralized, and targeted poverty reduction programs; and economic management and statistical systems. The new focus on states willing to reform has led to Bank support for two comprehensive reform programs in Andhra Pradesh, Karnataka, and Uttar Pradesh, and close engagement with Orissa and Rajasthan.

But lending commitments of $2.1 billion in fiscal 1998 were much lower than planned because of the sanctions imposed by major Bank shareholders after India's nuclear testing in May 1998. Under the sanctions, only projects meeting a "basic human needs" criterion were allowed to go forward. At the end of 1999 the sanctions had

---

Box 2.2   Poverty Reduction Focus of Bank Assistance

A clear Bank assistance strategy for poverty reduction in India did not emerge until the late 1990s. The 1997 Country Assistance Strategy (CAS) contained the first explicit proposals for Bank assistance (Annex 2 of the CAS) to address poverty on all three fronts suggested by *World Development Report 1990*. The 1999 CAS progress report reaffirmed this approach.

There is now considerable energy devoted to ensuring the poverty focus of Bank operations. In addition to continuing to address policy and infrastructural constraints to growth and to support improved social services, the Bank approved more targeted poverty interventions in Andhra Pradesh and Rajasthan through District Poverty Initiative projects and is planning such a project in Madhya Pradesh. These projects have the characteristics of social funds with the addition of significant institutional development components. They rely on existing institutional struc-

tures to support communities to identify, design, and implement projects that communities demand and then maintain. In short, they aim at developing community and village social capital as a way of making faster progress in poverty reduction among the poorest groups. A formal but simple ex-ante evaluation procedure, designed to forestall corruption, uses village councils, or *Gram Panchayats*, for review, and then processing by a district office for approval and close monitoring.

The World Bank Quality Assurance Group review of these projects in 1999 noted some risk that the institutional framework may not be sustained, but regarded them as carefully prepared, with sound quality at entry and strong government support, and therefore well worth trying. As these projects can become models for nationwide poverty reduction programs, implementation should be closely watched.

held up more than $2 billion of IBRD lending for energy, state roads, and other infrastructure projects.

In the January 1999 CAS progress report, the Bank recognized that India had not met the 1997 CAS fiscal triggers and had made only limited progress in structural reform. Thus India was at the border "between the base case and the low case, still in the former but heading in the direction of the latter." Consistently, India ex-pected a lending envelope for fiscal 1999 of $1.9 billion. Because sanctions remained in place, blocking all the infrastructure projects in the pipeline, only $1.1 billion was committed in fiscal 1999. In fiscal 2000 the sanctions were de facto relaxed in the fourth quarter, but the Bank still committed only $1.8 billion, remaining on the border between the base case ($2.7–3 billion) and the low case ($1.2 billion) lending scenarios presented to the Board a year earlier.

THE BANK'S PRODUCTS AND SERVICES

Analytical Services: High Quality but Limited Outreach

Through the mid-1990s, poverty-focused Bank research assessed poverty trends and the factors that influenced them. This high-quality work was appreciated in Indian academic circles. In the late 1990s Bank research focused more on the impact of different policies on poverty reduction and thus became more relevant to policymakers.

Country Economic Memoranda (CEMs), sector reports (for example, in transport, education, health, and so on), and Poverty Assessments synthesized research findings of the Bank and others and analyzed most of the relevant issues. (Although the policy framework in agriculture was only addressed in the later part of the 1990s.) The CEMs became a vehicle to discuss macroeconomic policies and sector policies. The 1992 CEM took an in-depth view of the structural reforms under way and the shortcomings of poverty alleviation programs. The 1993 CEM raised for the first time issues related to state finances. The 1994 CEM dealt with issues of capital controls and recommended the Chilean example of taxation on potentially volatile inflows, generating considerable controversy with the International Monetary Fund (IMF) at a time when this idea was not popular. The 1995 CEM went into more detail on state finances and legal reform.

Typically, the Bank also took a less alarming view of India's fiscal deficits and worked on the basis of a much higher sustainable fiscal deficit than the IMF did. Interestingly, because India's growth performance exceeded Bank and IMF forecasts, actual sustainable deficits were even higher than the estimates. Many of the themes and issues raised in the Bank's CEMs found their way into the Ministry of Finance's annual economic surveys and the Reserve Bank of India's annual reports—suggesting the Bank had at least an indirect impact on the intellectual debate on policies.

But Bank reports have been cautious in presenting conclusions and policy options (see box 4.1) because of the government's sensitivity to criticism, its resistance to policy advice from external sources, and its view that Indian experts and officials should be left to draw their own conclusions on policy issues. As a result the dissemination of controversial analyses and recommendations has often been restricted, and many Bank reports have not been processed for final distribution to the Board.[1] Recently, dis-

Box 3.1	The Bank's Outreach Has Improved but Still Falls Short

Strengthening of the Bank's outreach efforts in the 1990s took place in a favorable environment created by the new Indian consensus on economic reforms, the collapse of the socialist experiment in Eastern Europe, and China's opening and liberalization. The Bank's policy of greater openness and disclosure has been highly beneficial for both India and the Bank, and has helped the Bank evolve into a provider of knowledge beyond the confines of the Indian bureaucracy. The Bank grasped the rich dissemination opportunities of the Internet by putting a large amount of material online and by expanding its contacts with the popular, electronic, and foreign media. Greater contact and collaboration with local academics and nongovernmental organizations has im-

proved information flow and built bridges and local capacity. As a consequence, the Bank's image improved greatly in the 1990s.

But the Bank's in-country external relations efforts have not been sufficiently proactive and effective, partly because of limited human, budget, and management support. Bank dissemination has overemphasized new loans and lending volumes and has been mainly targeted to English-language print media. In a still mostly rural country with high illiteracy rates, the Bank needs to make a greater effort to reach the vernacular press and to harness the potential of television, especially in local languages. Recent staff additions and a larger budget promise improvement in outreach.

semination has improved, but further progress is possible (see box 3.1).

Eight of nine reports that the Bank's Quality Assurance Group (QAG) panels reviewed were rated satisfactory (the Bankwide average is 72 percent), and one was proposed for best practice (see box 3.2). All received positive comments on strategic relevance, technical aspects, and timeliness. But links among strategic goals, policy dialogue, and economic and sector work design and findings were lacking. Some reports didn't meet other criteria, such as realistic, measurable objectives (environmental issues, rural development); presentation, with emphasis on key recommendations and policy options (urban infrastructure, rural development, water resources, poverty); likely impact (water resources); and cost effectiveness (urban infrastructure, environmental issues, water resource management).

Most Bank reports appear to have little direct impact, reflecting their limited scope and dissemination, the variety and richness of intellectual contributions within India, and the drawn-out internal consensus-building and decisionmaking processes. Yet some exceptions stand out: the Bank's policy work in the late 1980s on trade and investment liberalization influenced the pace and extent of reform in the early 1990s, according to its Indian architects. The new crop of state economic reports also appears to have had a significant impact through highly relevant analyses of fiscal, struc-

tural, policy, and institutional deficiencies undertaken in close partnership with local policy institutes. Similarly, the most recent economic report is highly relevant, high in quality, and deserving of wide dissemination (World Bank 2000).[2]

The Bank also made excellent use in India of some of its global sector work. The foundations of the assistance program in education were the 1990 Jomtien Conference on Education for All and the economic and sector work prepared for it. The health program was built on the strength of the Bank's global work on disease priorities and the *1993 World Development Report*. The Bank involved Indian experts in the preparations for the Jomtien conference and the report. The Bank also organized high-level workshops in the country, in cooperation with local institutes and with the participation of some of the best primary education and disease and health systems experts in the world.

Lending Priorities: Toward Social Sectors

The Bank's lending shifted in the 1990s toward health, education, and social protection. A new Bank management team, saddled with a portfolio weak in both relevance and implementation, proceeded to a deep restructuring that entailed massive cancellations and staff redeployment. In fiscal 1990–94 the team cancelled projects amounting to $3.2 billion, a large portion in energy, compared with $0.4 billion during the pre-

Box 3.2	A Strong Link Between Analysis and Policy Dialogue

A Quality Assurance Group review panel has praised the report *Uttar Pradesh: From Fiscal Crisis to Renewed Growth* (World Bank 1998) and proposed it for best practice on all criteria (relevance, internal quality, presentation, and likely impact) for reasons such as the following:

- The state government initiated the study request without any prodding by Bank staff.
- The Bank assembled a high-caliber team with an appropriate skill mix.
- The study was undertaken jointly by Bank staff and state officials who felt like equal partners.
- Co-task management proved very useful in interactions with the client in Delhi and the sectoral specialists in Washington.
- The country director provided strong leadership and support in the dialogue with the client, adequately resourced the task, and steered the report internally.

- The study's context, objectives, and scope were clear in the minds of Bank management and task team leaders and shared by the state officials.
- The report integrated sector knowledge and perspective into the macroeconomic and fiscal framework consistently and coherently and tailored them to the state's circumstances.
- The recommendations were tested for their political feasibility by involving the politicians.
- The strategy for report dissemination respected political sensitivities, but also made sure to reach out beyond bureaucratic circles. The state published and circulated the recommendations in a suitable fashion, which muted opposition to the recommendations as being pushed by the Bank.

vious five years. Cancellations were still high in fiscal 1995–2000, at $1.1 billion.

Agriculture remained the largest sector at about 16 percent of new commitments in fiscal 1996–2000, even after experiencing a decline due to a review of lending for irrigation in the first half of the 1990s. Within the sector, irrigation remained dominant, but lending for broad-based rural development increased. From virtually nil in the 1980s, lending for health and nutrition, education, and social development expanded dramatically (to 35 percent) because of the government's changed attitude toward Bank involvement in these areas. Transport increased its share, but power and urban development were virtually phased out. In the power sector this resulted from the Bank's insistence since 1993 that lending be conditional on far-reaching policy and institutional changes. In the urban sector, the Bank took a decade-long pause to reflect on the failures of the past. Lending for industry and oil and gas disappeared altogether as the private sector took over (see figure 3.1).

As of June 1998, 73 percent of the Bank's outstanding portfolio ($12.9 billion) was earmarked for state governments and other beneficiaries identifiable by state. Of the lending commitments going to states, more than half were for high-poverty states, roughly mirror-

ing the geographical distribution of the poor (see figure 3.2).

Completed Project Performance: Mediocre

The 121 completed and evaluated operations in fiscal 1991–2000 (for a total of $18 billion in net commitments), three quarters of which were approved during the 1980s, had mixed results. OED rated only 72 percent of commitments satisfactory for outcome, 58 percent likely to be sustainable, and 38 percent substantial in institutional development impact—all below Bankwide averages.

Among the 28 projects completed and evaluated in the most recent three years (fiscal 1998–2000, with $4.2 billion in commitments), virtually all of which were initiated in the 1990s, performance was significantly improved across the board. For outcome, 74 percent of commitments were satisfactory; 65 percent carried likely sustainability ratings, and 44 percent had a substantial institutional development impact—all still below Bankwide averages but in line with International Development Association (IDA) and blend countries' performance (see table 3.1 and figure 3.3). Of nine projects evaluated during 2000, one is a top-rated project (Technician Education II, see box 4.4); seven show a satisfactory outcome, al-

Figure 3.1	Net Lending Commitments by Sector, 1986–90 and 1996–2000

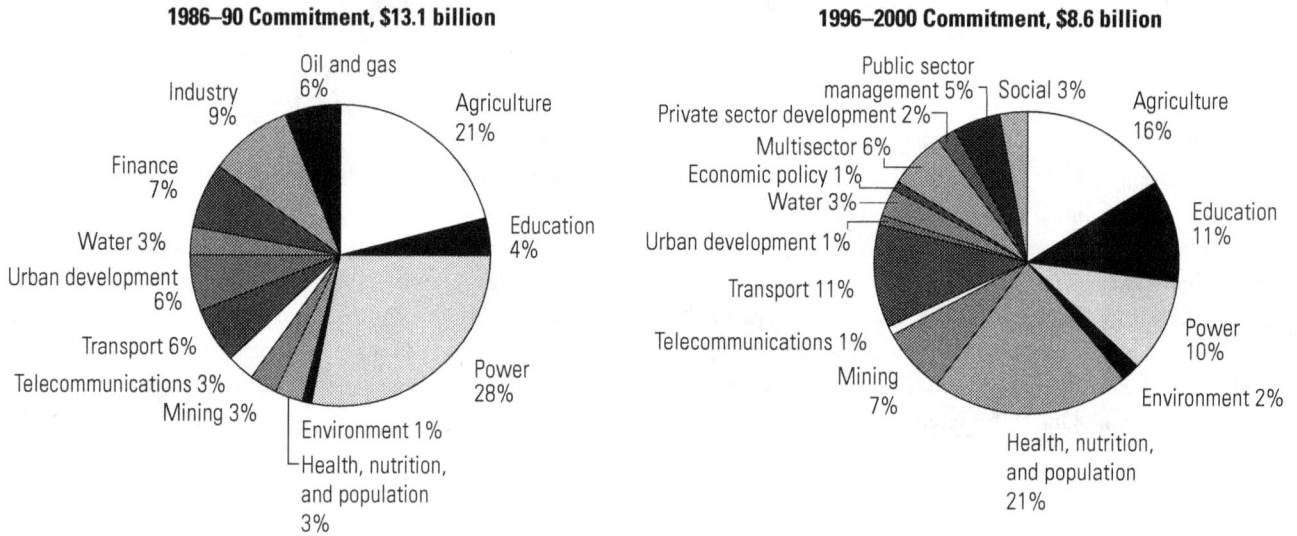

1986–90 Commitment, $13.1 billion

Oil and gas 6%
Industry 9%
Finance 7%
Water 3%
Urban development 6%
Transport 6%
Telecommunications 3%
Mining 3%
Environment 1%
Health, nutrition, and population 3%
Agriculture 21%
Education 4%
Power 28%

1996–2000 Commitment, $8.6 billion

Public sector management 5%
Private sector development 2%
Multisector 6%
Economic policy 1%
Water 3%
Urban development 1%
Transport 11%
Telecommunications 1%
Mining 7%
Social 3%
Agriculture 16%
Education 11%
Power 10%
Environment 2%
Health, nutrition, and population 21%

Source: World Bank data.

Figure 3.2	India's Poverty Distribution and Bank Lending

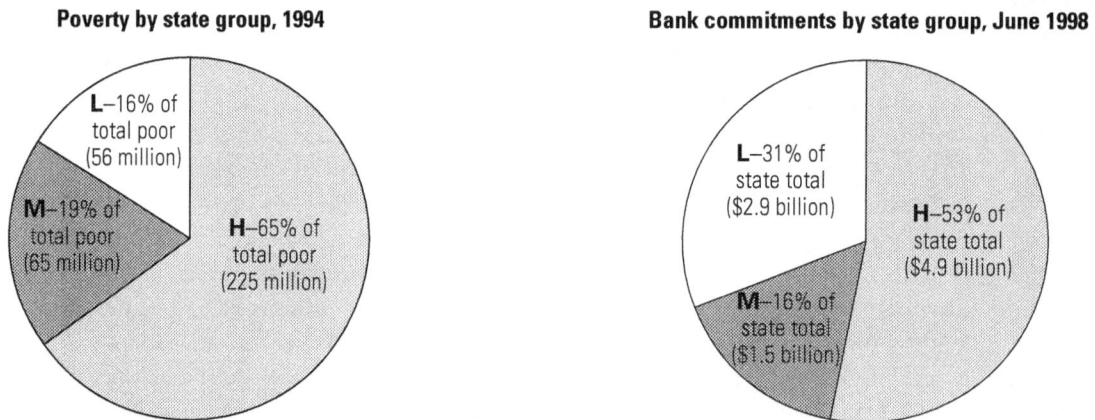

Poverty by state group, 1994

L–16% of total poor (56 million)
M–19% of total poor (65 million)
H–65% of total poor (225 million)

Bank commitments by state group, June 1998

L–31% of state total ($2.9 billion)
M–16% of state total ($1.5 billion)
H–53% of state total ($4.9 billion)

H = high absolute poverty states (number of poor greater than 30 million: Bihar, Madhya Pradesh, Maharashtra, Uttar Pradesh).
M = medium absolute poverty states (number of poor greater than 12 million: Andhra Pradesh, Karnataka, Orissa, Rajasthan, Tamil Nadu, West Bengal).
L = low absolute poverty states (number of poor less than 12 million: all others).

Source: World Bank data.

though one (the Dam Safety project) received a modest institutional development impact rating; and one (the Industrial Pollution Control project) received a moderately unsatisfactory rating.

Completed project performance indicators based on number of projects (see table 3.1) and on the economic rates of return (a quarter of those projects for which such rate was calculated had economic rates of return less than 10 percent) point to a similar picture. Water supply and sanitation, agriculture, finance, power, and the environment were the worst-performing sectors, while social sectors, industry, and oil and gas were the best (see table 3.2).

Monitoring and evaluation (M&E) arrangements to track the poverty reduction and gender impact of Bank projects and government programs, with few exceptions, have been weak (see the Country Assistance Evaluation poverty, rural, gender, and environment background papers). But the Bank has begun to correct this inadequacy in recently approved projects. For instance, the District Poverty Initiative projects include provision for baseline surveys, regular collection of monitoring information during implementation, and quick analysis and evaluation of this information, to provide the basis for any changes in the programs as they proceed. Similarly, the Uttar Pradesh Health Systems Development project has identified explicit achievement targets for the general population, the poor, and women and has provisions for M&E of performance. Finally, thorough and comprehensive M&E arrangements have been put in place in the context of the comprehensive adjustment program supported by the Bank in Uttar Pradesh, including a baseline, state-specific poverty assessment. Moreover, the June 2000 workshop on "Poverty Monitoring and Evaluation" organized by the Bank's Poverty Reduction and Economic Management Network and the regional office has been an important step forward in strengthening M&E arrangements in India.

Quality at entry—relevance, design, and preparedness—for the Bank's completed projects in

Table 3.1	OED Project Evaluation Ratings, Comparative Performance, Various Fiscal Years					
Area/period	Number of projects	Net commitment (US$ millions)	Satisfactory outcome (percent)	Likely sustainability (percent)	Substantial institutional development impact (percent)	Satisfactory Bank performance at appraisal (percent)
India, 1981–90	107	9,785	72 / 72	47 / 53	18 / 26	55 / 65
1991–2000	121	18,033	68 / 72	47 / 58	36 / 38	56 / 62
1996–2000	50	7,703	68 / 71	58 / 65	40 / 37	56 / 54
1998–2000	28	4,222	71 / 74	57 / 65	46 / 44	68 / 63
Sri Lanka, 1996–2000	18	623	67 / 72	50 / 66	22 / 21	56 / 69
Pakistan, 1996–2000	34	3,506	71 / 72	44 / 43	32 / 24	58 / 60
China, 1996–2000	46	6,239	85 / 88	78 / 81	65 / 69	74 / 76
East Asia and Pacific Region, 1996–2000	172	24,899	80 / 87	60 / 72	45 / 43	72 / 82
IDA and blend, 1996–2000	570	26,560	69 / 77	46 / 56	35 / 38	59 / 65
1998–2000	342	14,774	69 / 74	47 / 56	35 / 40	57 / 62
Bankwide, 1991–2000	2,254	167,589	69 / 77	49 / 61	34 / 41	64 / 72
1996–2000	1,095	88,646	72 / 80	53 / 63	39 / 45	63 / 73
1998–2000	637	52,757	73 / 82	55 / 68	41 / 49	62 / 75

Note: Includes all projects completed in fiscal 2000 and evaluated as of December 31, 2000. Numbers separated by slashes are percentage by number of projects and net commitment by exit years.

Figure 3.3	OED Project Evaluation Ratings by Commitment, Fiscal 1976-2000

Percent

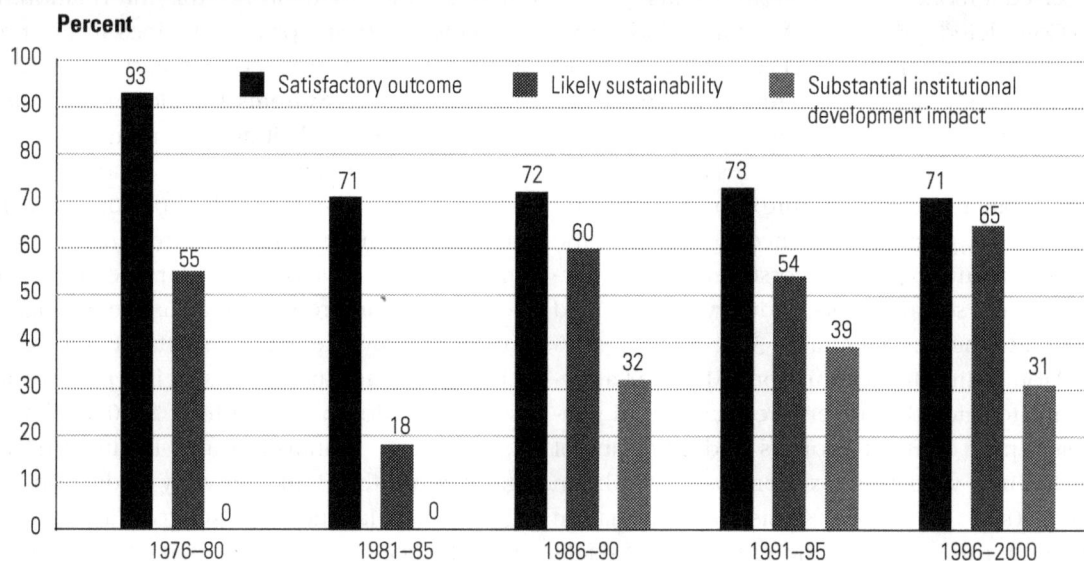

Note: Of the 40 projects evaluated by OED for fiscal 1976–80 exit, only 2 were rated for institutional development impact. Of the 44 projects evaluated for fiscal 1981–85, only 12 were rated for institutional development impact.
Source: OED database, December 2000.

Table 3.2	OED Project Evaluation Ratings, Sectoral Performance, Fiscal 1996-2000

Sector	Number of projects	Net commitment (US$ millions)	Satisfactory outcome (percent)	Likely sustainability (percent)	Substantial institutional development impact (percent)	Satisfactory Bank performance at appraisal (percent)
Agriculture	10	1,234	60 / 56	30 / 36	40 / 41	50 / 44
Education	3	576	100 / 100	100 / 100	67 / 80	67 / 80
Electric and power	8	1,849	50 / 58	38 / 47	25 / 32	50 / 49
Environment	4	339	75 / 59	50 / 34	50 / 34	50 / 34
Finance	3	433	67 / 57	67 / 57	67 / 57	67 / 57
Industry	2	431	100 / 100	100 / 100	100 / 100	100 / 100
Mining	2	308	50 / 96	50 / 96	50 / 3	0 / 0
Oil and gas	1	450	100 / 100	100 / 100	0 / 0	0 / 0
Health, nutrition, and population	7	625	86 / 88	86 / 89	29 / 22	100 / 100
Transport	3	513	67 / 64	67 / 64	0 / 0	33 / 48
Urban development	3	582	67 / 81	67 / 81	33 / 37	67 / 81
Water and sanitation	4	362	50 / 38	50 / 52	50 / 38	25 / 20
Total India	**50**	**7,703**	**68 / 71**	**58 / 65**	**40 / 37**	**56 / 54**

Note: Includes all projects completed in fiscal 2000 and evaluated as of December 31, 2000. Numbers separated by slashes are percentages by number of projects and net commitment by exit years.
Source: OED data.

India during the 1990s (proxied by OED ratings of Bank performance at appraisal) was poor in both absolute and relative terms. Only 56 percent of the 50 evaluated projects in fiscal 1996–2000 obtained satisfactory appraisal ratings, compared with 61 percent in fiscal 1990–94. Performance in the last three years has improved, but is still low. Quality at entry was particularly poor in the sectors mentioned above, but satisfactory in most projects in the health and education sectors. Several implementation problems, chiefly procurement delays, also undermined performance. The 1997 portfolio review noted the most common causes: weaknesses in preparing bid documents and in contracting procedures, and delays in contract awards following bid evaluation. Other problems included scarcity of counterpart funding and rapid turnover in the Bank's and borrower's project staff.

Ongoing Portfolio: Sound

Approval of 10 new projects in the fourth quarter of fiscal 2000 boosted the Bank's portfolio for India to 76 projects amounting to commitments of about $12.9 billion, with a high undisbursed balance of $8.0 billion. Based on the supervision ratings and QAG's classification, 29 percent of the commitments were at risk, a level higher than the previous peak in fiscal 1993 (28 percent) and considerably worse than the Bankwide level (16 percent). Commitment at risk doubled from the previous year, but this indicator is very volatile on a quarterly basis, precluding a strong conclusion. In fact, by end-December 2000, portfolio performance appears much improved, with only 9 percent of commitments at risk. However, the high historical disconnect ratio (19 percent in fiscal 1997–99, compared with 9 percent Bankwide and 19 percent for India in fiscal 1994–96) between Bank and OED completion ratings suggests a strong upward bias in self-evaluations.

QAG reviewed the quality at entry of two ongoing projects in 1999 (among 80 randomly selected Bankwide), one of which (the Andhra Pradesh Power project) was rated highly satisfactory; the other (the Rajasthan District Primary Education project), satisfactory. Similarly, of the two projects (among the 100 selected Bankwide)

reviewed in 1998, one (the Haryana Power Sector Restructuring project) was on the top 10 highly satisfactory list and the other (the Woman and Child Development project) was rated marginally satisfactory. A similar review of seven other India projects in 1997 found one highly satisfactory (the Coal Sector Rehabilitation project, scoring high on all QAG criteria) and one marginally satisfactory (the Rural Women's Development project).[3]

Efficiency: Adequate

Decentralization

In fiscal 1991 the resident mission was already responsible for a significant part of supervision work. In the following years its role expanded to encompass all of supervision, support for procurement, disbursement, and auditing, and to deal with strategic and policy issues related to infrastructure development, social development, public affairs, and state focus. The Bank's July 1997 reorganization created a matrix management structure with a small country management unit headed by a director posted in the field office and virtually all operational staff working on India placed administratively under regional sector unit managers (based at headquarters). The size of the field office increased from 50 to 57 professionals between fiscal 1991 and 1997 and jumped to 83 professionals by fiscal 1999 to implement the decentralization objective of the strategic compact.

Preliminary estimates from a study of total field office costs currently under way as part of a Bankwide review show that in fiscal 1999 the India field office spent about $8 million, or 24 percent, of the South Asia Region's expenditures on the whole India program. This is about the same percentage as for Africa and slightly lower than for the East Asia and Pacific Region (26 percent). South Asia's expenditures for the entire India program for fiscal 1999 ($33 million) represented about 5 percent of the total for all Regions, a much lower percentage than the country's share of the developing world's population or the poor.

Expanded field presence was critical to the successful expansion of Bank assistance in education and social development and for enhancing the state focus of assistance. The shrinking field presence in agriculture and gender paralleled less successful performances in these areas. Bank staff and OED evaluators with exposure to the Bank's activities in India have praised the Bank's enhanced appreciation of country culture and conditions and the client focus that decentralization has brought about. A client survey conducted in 1998 reflected satisfaction with the impact of decentralization, especially more nimble decisionmaking and greater resilience of the Bank-India partnership. Clients seek even more delegation of authority to field office staff.

Cost and Efficiency Indicators

The trend in the Bank's total staff direct costs for India has been flat since fiscal 1995 at about $16 million, up by about 9 percent compared with the early 1990s. India's economic and sector work and lending unit costs, which were generally lower than for China in fiscal 1990–94, rose substantially in the second half of the decade, and were well above recent unit costs for China and East Asia and Pacific programs, which instead decreased over the same period. Project preparation costs in India were also higher than those for other large countries, including Argentina, Brazil, and Mexico. Supervision costs, in contrast, compared favorably even with large countries, and lending costs per commitment dollar were substantially lower than for neighboring Pakistan and other Regions, reflecting the economies of scale of India's larger average project size.[4]

Available operational efficiency measures are highly imperfect but point to average performance. During fiscal 1995–99 India's total program costs per satisfactory commitment dollar were 41 percent higher than China's and 18–90 percent higher than those for other larger countries in Latin America and the Caribbean. But India's costs were slightly lower than those for East Asia and Pacific and Latin America and the Caribbean and substantially lower than those in all other Regions. Moreover, the performance of the outstanding portfolio has seen notable improvement. Finally, indicators of service efficiency up to fiscal 1999 compared well with

China and the two Asian Regions and were also close to Bank service standards.

Aid Coordination and Effectiveness: Uneven

Aid coordination and mobilization have been pursued through regular annual donor meetings outside India, at which the government and Bank have solicited pledges to fill the external financing gap estimated by government and Bank economists. In addition, the United Nations Development Programme chairs various sectoral in-country working groups.

Aid coordination among donors has been minimal at the country-strategy level and uneven at the subsectoral and state levels (for example, it has been strong in health but neglected in agriculture). Moreover, partnerships with other donors appear to be declining.[5] Even coordination internal to the Bank Group has been suboptimal. Indeed, the Bank–International Finance Corporation (IFC) 1997 Country Assistance Strategy was a one-sided Bank document. The Bank's efforts at encouraging private sector participation in infrastructure (in power, for example) were not sufficiently coordinated with the IFC until recently.[6]

According to a 1998 client survey, government officials appreciate the Bank's deference to the government's preeminent role in aid coordination. A survey of the main donors, conducted in May/June 1999 for this evaluation, suggests that they would appreciate a more active Bank role. For donors the goal of mobilizing resources appears to be less important than interacting with partners about the country's development priorities; addressing environmental, poverty, and governance issues; and encouraging civil society, nongovernmental organizations, and the private sector to participate in the country's development.[7] The respondents thought that the relevance and impact of aid coordination activities with respect to the balance of payments, governance issues, and financial and private sector development were low or negligible. Their responses to questions on outputs and impact of aid coordination indicate only modest achievements, ambivalence about the government's ability to coordinate aid, and a desire for a more active Bank role, especially in-country. This mismatch suggests the need for an intensive dialogue (led by the government) among all India's external partners about aid coordination arrangements and the role of the Bank.

The major lessons from country program evaluations by three donors (Swiss Agency for Development Cooperation, the government of the Netherlands, and the Department for International Development) confirm the importance of several factors for the success of external assistance:

- Adequacy of the policy and institutional environment
- Client ownership, commitment, and appropriate design, which are facilitated (and tested) by the use of pilot projects, beneficiary participation, and local partnerships (see boxes 2.1 and 4.4)
- Quality at entry, through simplicity of design and early identification of institutional capacity constraints
- Attention to gender concerns
- Investment in knowledge products combining foreign and local expertise as the most effective way to influence decisionmakers.

4

SELECTED SECTORS AND TOPICS

Overview of Sectoral Assistance

The effectiveness of Bank assistance during the 1990s varied among sectors. Results have been strongest in power (in the second half of the decade). They have been good in private sector development, population, health, nutrition, and education and modest elsewhere.[1]

Public Sector Management

Fiscal adjustment and public enterprise reform were supported by the 1991 structural adjustment loan, but with little long-term impact. Together with the other two projects of the early 1990s (the External Sector and the Social Safety Net adjustment operations), the Bank supported institutional changes in taxation; the financial sector; and the trade, foreign exchange, and investment regimes. Since explicitly acknowledging the seriousness of governance problems in the December 1997 Country Assistance Strategy (CAS), the Bank has paid much more attention to this issue in both its lending and nonlending activities. Civil service issues are beginning to be addressed in the focus states. The Bank's economic and sector work on public sector management, while inconsequential at the center, is having a stronger impact at the state level. Fiscal and public enterprise reform issues are also being addressed in the context of state-level, policy-based lending.

Institutional development components of projects were more focused at the agency level (and even here, narrowly so, mostly in skill upgrad-

ing and management) than broadly at the sector, state, or national levels. Results were modest. Only 16 out of 100 projects completed in India and reviewed by OED in a 1997 survey had a primary focus on institutional development. In the face of weak line institutions, the Bank relied on project implementation units to ensure better project performance, but this has been at the expense of strengthening or reforming the existing institutional machinery.

Financial and Private Sector Development

The Bank's high-quality economic and sector work, intensive policy dialogue, and lending operations (including the three adjustment loans) in the early 1990s were relevant and contributed effectively and in a timely way to good progress in the incentives framework facing the private sector and to strengthening the financial system. India's commitment to structural adjustment in 1991 represented a clear breakthrough from the piecemeal approach to policy change.

In the second half of the decade, however, a Bank loan supporting the restructuring of a small number of public banks achieved very little and had virtually no demonstration effect on the rest of the banking system. But the Bank's strong advisory role helped maintain the momentum of the financial sector reforms. Moreover, many impediments to private sector growth remain unaddressed, such as labor market rigidities, delayed justice, poor corporate governance, slow and ineffective privatization of public enterprises and banks, and lack of private sector participation in the development of ports and roads. These are areas where the policy dialogue could have been more forceful.

Urban Development

The Bank has not finalized an urban development strategy, even after a major but protracted sector study and evaluation of its unsatisfactory experience in the 1980s. There has been virtually no new lending during the 1990s, except for water supply and sanitation projects. But the reach of the eight projects completed and evaluated has been limited, and in most cases the borrowers' weak commitment to the agreed pricing and institutional reforms meant that even their limited outcomes were not sustainable. In spite of 25 years of Bank assistance for urban water supply projects, no Indian city today can provide safe water for more than a few hours a day, and most water and sanitation agencies have financial difficulties and offer inadequate service.

Relevance of sectoral assistance has been improving in the late 1990s, but remains modest. Three ongoing projects are being implemented satisfactorily, according to the latest progress reports. But they are narrowly focused on specific cities rather than on sectorwide issues and municipal development. Furthermore, there has been little follow-up by the Bank on its 1996 sector work (which the Quality Assurance Group, QAG, judged "an outstanding piece of analytical work") for building the capacity of municipalities, helping the central government and other tiers of government implement the urban agenda, and fostering a better balance between private and public participation.

Agriculture and Rural Development

The Bank's 1991 country economic report concluded that Indian agriculture was in crisis, largely brought about by serious policy and institutional shortcomings at the central and state government levels. Given the importance of agricultural and rural development to economic growth and poverty reduction, adjustments in agricultural sector policy deserved to be pursued within the government's broader program of stabilization and reform. Despite the report's conclusions, agricultural policy issues were never near the top of the Bank's strategic agenda during the first half of the 1990s. Since there was a similar lack of interest on the government side, the Bank made only weak attempts at meaningful dialogue on agricultural policy. This neglect also held up further analytical work by the Bank on Indian agriculture and weakened the relevance of its sectoral assistance.

Compared with the late 1980s, there was a reduction in Bank lending for agriculture in the first half of the 1990s, largely due to a review of the dominant irrigation lending component rather than a response to the unsatisfactory policy environment in the sector. Nonetheless, the Bank continued to lend substantial amounts in the sector in an overregulated and inefficient policy environment, with many stand-alone projects addressing relatively narrow issues. In a few states the Bank sought adjustments in agricultural policy, with some success (for example, in water pricing). But such efforts were often undermined by weak enforcement of the hard-won project covenants, while large-scale lending continued.

The Bank's assistance program was also slow to adjust to changing circumstances. For example, the extension system assisted by a Bank-funded project was geared mainly to supporting irrigated grain production rather than diversified and rainfed agriculture, which would have been more relevant for rural poverty reduction. Earlier extension projects also used the discredited training and visit system, but revised extension models are being explored in two recently approved projects (the National Agricultural Technology and the Uttar Pradesh Diversified Agricultural Support projects).

In the second half of the 1990s lending for agriculture and rural development increased, but the

Bank concentrated on a few main subsectors and placed even more emphasis on state-level reforms. The new, sharper focus of assistance arose from the realization that earlier neglect of agricultural policy issues and dispersion of projects had limited sustainable impact on poverty reduction and were creating serious problems in project implementation and performance. The increased lending was for irrigation and drainage (still the dominant part of the portfolio), watershed and area development, and forestry. There were also project components directed at agricultural research and extension. Overall, Bank lending was largely directed to states willing to adopt significant policy reforms, such as for water management and pricing. This more selective and relevant sector orientation had a larger impact on rural development institutions than the disparate and enclave projects of earlier years.

Providing the rural poor (mostly landless peasants or farmers on marginal lands) with access to land on a formal basis—rather than through often illegal tenancy arrangements—and more off-farm employment opportunities, which in recent years have increased slowly, is important for sustained poverty reduction (World Bank 2000). Over the past few years the Bank has indeed focused more on the assetless rural

poor, although the majority of the ongoing rural development projects still favor those with such assets as land. Bank researchers have recently argued in favor of the need for agrarian reform in India, including improved land distribution (Mearns 1999; Mearns and Sinha 1999). Nevertheless, for enhanced off-farm (as well as on-farm) employment opportunities for the poor, boosting agricultural production remains critical because "the greatest stimulant for growth of the nonagricultural economy in rural areas is dynamic agricultural growth" (Fisher, Mahajan, and Singha 1997). Such a boost in the sector's growth, in turn, will require substantial policy improvements.

In 1999 the Bank concluded a major review of rural development and poverty reduction that had begun in the mid-1990s with the commissioning of subsector reviews. The review culminated in a good synthesis report that pointed to substantial shortcomings in incentives, institutions, and public expenditure priorities. The report, however, should have taken a bolder approach by presenting more specific recommendations (see box 4.1). India is defining its sectoral assistance strategy in light of this sector work. The Bank has not made clear how it intends to strengthen focus on agricultural and rural development policy in its future policy dialogue,

---

Box 4.1   Cautious Conclusions Cloud the Policy Dialogue for Rural Development

A Quality Assurance Group (QAG) review panel found that *India – Towards Rural Development and Poverty Reduction* (World Bank 1999b), as a synthesis, contains much good analytical material. And the thrust of the report's conclusions and recommendations is sound. But it presents surprisingly timid recommendations for changes in incentives, institutions, and investments.

The panel acknowledged the report's strong points, which included its synthesis of existing but unexploited analytical work and its discussion of sequencing of proposed policy changes (quite a rarity). In line with the rural development strategy advocated in *Rural Development: From Vision to Action* (World Bank 1997), it addresses rural, not just agricultural, development; poverty reduction in its widest dimensions (except for land redistribution); and desirable changes in incentive regimes, institutional arrangements, and public investment.

The QAG panel thought that the Bank should have taken a bolder approach by being more specific on recommendations for reductions of subsidies for canal irrigation, power, and urea. And by leveraging its lending on corresponding actions (although best handled separately). Nonetheless, the renewed interest of the Indian government to review its agricultural policies and rural development strategy led the panel to a positive assessment of the report's likely impact.

The Country Assistance Evaluation sectoral background review also concluded that the report could have been bolder in presenting its conclusions and that its impact on crucial issues for rural development and the poor remains uncertain. The report was discussed at a workshop in New Delhi and later with the government, but no further dissemination in the states had been initiated by the end of 2000.

in its overall country strategy, and in its operations at the central and state government levels.[2]

Lending in the irrigation subsector had been a crucial part of the Bank's support for increased grain production based on Green Revolution technology, which depended heavily on irrigation. Through the 1990s, this lending still accounted for about 50 percent of the agricultural portfolio. Since early in the decade, Bank assistance has been mostly for river basin development through the state-focused Water Resource Consolidation projects in the context of increasing pressures on domestic, agricultural, and industrial water demand. Major objectives were to improve river basin planning and water management to increase the reliability of water supplies and support higher agricultural productivity. These projects were also intended to help complete a number of older projects whose implementation had stalled.

But these projects focused too much on construction and not enough on institutional reform and water management. Also, irrigation projects continued to be implemented in a policy environment providing the wrong incentives for water use and agricultural production. Results have been disappointing so far. Only half of the 18 projects completed in the 1990s have been rated satisfactory, only a third were judged to have had substantial institutional development impact, and only three were evaluated as having likely sustainability (for an example of a failed project, see box 4.2).

In the second half of the 1990s, following the release of a global water resources policy paper by the Bank (but at the same time as the Bank's review of irrigation strategy for India in 1998), the Bank's irrigation assistance has focused increasingly on strengthening the institutional capacity of irrigation management systems, establishing water users associations, and recovering costs for irrigation water. The new crop of projects appears to be performing much better than their forerunners.

**Box 4.2   An Extraordinary Failure—
The Upper Krishna Irrigation II Project**

Objectives. The Upper Krishna Irrigation II project (a $167 million International Development Association credit approved in 1989 and closed in mid-1997) had the commendable objective of increasing employment and incomes of 100,000 poor families in the arid north of Karnataka. It was to do this by developing 150,000 hectares of irrigation, including dam construction; resettling and improving the living standards of displaced persons; strengthening capacity in irrigation management; and contributing to an effective antimalaria campaign.

Weak Implementation. The physical objectives were only partially achieved (80 percent). While the plentiful availability of irrigation water at virtually zero cost to users has increased yields and returns by 200–400 percent, slow development of the command area and inefficient use of water resources has led to practically no net benefits to the project because of the substantial project cost. There are now no functioning water users associations, despite 50 having been created during 1990–92. Association members had stopped water rotation soon after the project delivered ample water, as they saw no reason to ration water and submit individual delivery preferences to group decisions. Moreover, the oversupply of water,

with considerable water logging, has caused serious damage to houses and crops.

For the state government, dam construction on the Krishna River was the priority. As a result, despite written assurances, dam construction took place and many villages were submerged without completion of the resettlement arrangements. Resettlement expenditures by the state government after closing the Bank's credit have been $166 million, compared with $101 million during the eight years of Bank assistance. This influx of funds, combined with improved administrative procedures and institutional capacity, has led to more resettled families using income-generating-scheme grants (from 12 percent to 16 percent), land purchase grants (from 16 percent to 29 percent), and house construction grants (from 33 percent to 51 percent).

Outcome and Lessons. Despite the late corrections to the resettlement component, this project had an unsatisfactory outcome and is unsustainable. The project provided three lessons: the Bank ignored its own agreement with the state government on the need for coordination between irrigation development and resettlement, water management reforms were not pursued, and supply-led irrigation development cannot be sustained.

The Uttar Pradesh Sodic Lands Reclamation project, for example, has not only been technically successful but has also created opportunities for women and the poor to access productive land and higher incomes (see box 4.3). Another example of the Bank's new approach is the ongoing irrigation component of the Andhra Pradesh Economic Restructuring project, which focuses on reducing the role of government and enhancing the role of beneficiaries in the management of major parts of irrigation systems. In three years there has been a remarkable improvement in rehabilitation of canals, water management, and cost recovery in Andhra Pradesh as a result of the empowerment of water users groups to manage the tertiary irrigation systems.

Improving the quality and quantity of rural water supplies is one of the important development challenges in India—on average only about 75 percent of the rural population has access to public water supplies, which leaves some 175 million people without safe public water. While many rural development projects also contain rural water supply components, the performance of two completed stand-alone projects in Maharashtra and Kerala was modestly satisfactory at best, but two other ongoing projects in Karnataka and Uttar Pradesh are progressing satisfactorily. The thrust of the ongoing Bank assistance—to improve health and pro-

ductivity by creating conditions at the state level for the sustainable supply of safe water through increased involvement of the private sector—is appropriate, as neither the Bank nor governments can possibly assist all rural areas directly.

Two watershed management projects (classified as environment projects) were approved in fiscal 1990 and implemented satisfactorily. They addressed watershed issues in the "plains" and the "hills" in a number of states. At the end of fiscal 1999 a second hills project—designed to intensify a participatory approach to implementation—was approved. A series of watershed projects is being planned, in contrast to area development projects, to reflect the idea that watersheds should be the organizing principle for area development in rural settings. While Bank assistance for rural roads has been relatively limited, it has been highly relevant and efficacious throughout the decade.

In the early 1990s the Bank launched a new program of assistance for the forestry sector based on the Government's policy statement of 1988 and the Bank's forestry policy paper of 1991. The Bank's policy (similar to the government's) was based on four principles: multisectoral approaches and international cooperation; rectifying market and policy failures that led to deforestation and unsustainable land use; financing operations that lead to socially, environmentally, and economically sustainable

---

Box 4.3 — **Strong Local Institutions and the Right Incentives: Uttar Pradesh Sodic Lands Projects**

The main objective of the two Uttar Pradesh Sodic Lands Reclamation projects (the first approved in 1993 and almost completed, and another approved in 1999) is to reclaim areas that have become contaminated with high levels of salt in the soil and were unproductive under previous water management regimes. Backed by the enthusiastic support of the state government, the approach involves large-scale drainage, use of chemicals, on-farm development, promotion of forest species on community lands, and strengthening local institutions so they can participate in implementing the land reclamation program. An important target group for the use of the reclaimed land is the poor and landless.

Very substantial benefits have come from crop diversification and increased crop yields, leading to an almost 50 percent increase in family income. Paddy yields have risen from 1.2 to 3.74 tons per hectare; wheat yields from 0.75 to 2.63 tons per hectare. About 11,138 hectares have been allocated to the landless (average farm size is about 0.5 hectare). Village implementation committees review and decide on land allocation. Women's self-help groups operate small-scale credit schemes.

Planned recovery of operation and maintenance costs will be only partial in the short term. But since most of the beneficiaries are poor and the farms are very small, this may be a better way to transfer resources to the poor.

resource expansion and intensification; and preserving intact forest areas.

In addition to the multistate Forestry Research, Education, and Extension project and the Ecodevelopment project, the Bank financed six state forestry projects in the 1990s that supported the development strategies of the state forest departments and also aimed at strengthening the capacity of the relevant state institutions. Much of the population living around forests is poor, and hence this assistance has an impact on poverty reduction through employment and the generation of productive assets.

There is considerable variation in the performance of these projects depending on the commitment of the state forestry agencies, but their main contributions have been to:

- Provide crucial additional financing for important state forestry programs that have generated employment for the poor.
- Strengthen local capacity for forest resource management.
- Improve forestry officials' attitudes toward community participation.
- Raise policy and institutional development issues for discussion among stakeholders.

Issues that need attention in future Bank assistance include expanding the role of the private sector, the revenue-raising capabilities of the forest sector, marketing nontimber forest products, clarifiying of the roles of the center and the states in forestry, and project sustainability.

Power

The poor performance of power projects and the post-1991 adjustment spirit led the Bank in 1993 to decide that new lending would be conditional on the adoption of far-reaching restructuring of the state electricity boards. The conditions included unbundling generation, transmission, and distribution; establishing an independent state regulatory authority; and privatizing all distribution facilities and all new generation investment. Since 1996 a new series of highly relevant power projects has emerged in a few states, with strong client ownership (Orissa, Haryana, Andhra Pradesh, Uttar Pradesh) and a substantial demonstration effect on others. A QAG review panel found the on-going Andhra Pradesh Power adaptable program loan ($210, approved in February 1999) highly satisfactory and noted that the Bank's sequential state-by-state approach yields opportunities for learning from experience across states with important cost savings. Both the OED sector evaluation and the QAG review panel concluded that the South Asia Region's approach in India is a best practice model that should be emulated throughout the Bank's energy sector portfolio.

Transport

The Bank's intrasector lending shift from a focus on railways in the 1980s to highways in the following decade was appropriate, given the government's unwillingness to address the railway's pricing distortions (with subsidies for passenger traffic financed by very high freight charges) and continuing poor corporate governance, exemplified by resistance to corporatizing (and eventually privatize) Indian Railway's large manufacturing units and social sector activities. At the same time, the government's decision in the mid-1980s to accept international competitive bidding procedures opened the door to highway lending. The increasing emphasis on subnational lending, however, has tilted the balance of sectoral assistance too much in favor of state projects, given that the national highway system represents only 8 percent of all major roads but carries 35 percent of the traffic and is the most congested.[3]

Environment

Since 1990 the Bank has lent $1.94 billion to India for 19 projects to mitigate environmental damage. Another $97 million was granted under Global Environment Facility and Montreal Protocol trust funds for four other projects to protect the global environment. The Bank has also supported various studies addressing environmental issues. According to OED interviews with stakeholders, the Bank's sector work has had considerable impact on policies and environmental awareness in the country. The Bank's most significant achievement is in mainstreaming environmental concerns in its agriculture, power, irrigation, and water supply and sanita-

Box 4.4 Best Practice Projects

Among the five dozen Bank-financed projects completed since fiscal 1995, six projects in five different sectors received the highest possible evaluation ratings, including highly satisfactory outcome. These projects were all very successful at achieving their physical and institutional strengthening objectives, but they differed greatly in their support for sectorwide policy and institutional change. OED has not yet audited these projects; it has only conducted brief desk reviews of the completion reports. The projects share a high degree of commitment, ownership, and long-term vision.

The *Oil India Ltd. Petroleum* project ($140 million, fiscal 1988–95) focused narrowly on maximizing oil recovery from declining oil fields in Assam. Components were limited to investment and improvements in technical and management capability for a committed and already financially viable public enterprise.

The *Industrial Technology* project ($200 million, fiscal 1990–98) was relevant in the pre- and post-liberalization environments. It catalyzed change, helped launch a domestic venture capital industry, attracted foreign venture capitalists, supported a stronger industry orientation, increased self-financing of technology research institutes, and contributed to liberalization of import policies. The project took into account market failures and distortions created by government import policies. Strong, committed intermediaries, flexible project design, strong financial incentives, consensus building, and training were crucial to success, allowing adaptation to the changing economic environment, changing technology institutions' attitudes, and creating new skills.

The two *Technician Education* projects ($472 million, fiscal 1991, fiscal 1998–00) were complex, multistate projects affecting the entire polytechnic system in 20 states and surpassing all physical and institutional targets, including women's enrollment (up to 30 percent from 11 percent before the projects). This includes making a new policy framework final in partnership with employers. Success factors are strong state ownership, frequent joint meetings and reviews fostering knowledge sharing among all states, a collegiate relationship among the Bank team and national and state counterparts, and full national policy support. Shortcomings are uneven state performance in adopting a flexible curriculum, instruction quality, and employer participation.

The *Private Power Utilities* project ($200 million, fiscal 1992–97) aimed to transform the Mumbai utility—majority-owned by three public financial institutions—from a distribution company into an integrated power utility. It also aimed to provide additional electricity capacity to meet increasing demand and to support efforts to transfer ownership to the private sector. Not devoid of controversy, preparation was delayed by a court action initiated by nongovernmental organizations on environmental grounds. Political commitment, ownership by the utility's management, and the company's financial strength and willingness to address the environmental implications proved key to the project's success.

In the *Maharashtra Emergency Earthquake Rehabilitation* project ($217 million, fiscal 1994–99), commitment, ownership, participation, long-term vision, and repair and reconstruction activities on an unprecedented scale succeeded in providing safe replacement dwellings for nearly 1 million people in the state's southeastern region. Vulnerability to seismic events was reduced by installing modern seismic equipment and preparing widely disseminated construction guidelines, a manual for nonengineered masonry construction, and a statewide disaster management plan.

---

tion portfolio. Substantial progress has been made lately on more rational power pricing in a few states that have embarked on Bank-supported reform. Price subsidies for water and energy producers and consumers, however, remain in most states and are highly damaging to the environment. Moreover, the overall impact of Bank and government actions to prevent environmental problems has been modest.

Environmental project performance has been mixed. Most forestry and water resource projects, the Uttar Pradesh Sodic Lands Reclamation project, and the Renewable Resources Development project, to cite a few, have performed well. Others, however, such as the Environmental Management Capacity Building project, the Bombay Sewage Disposal project, the Industrial Pollution Control project, and the Ecodevelopment project, have had difficulty in implementation for various reasons, including poor compliance by the borrowers, inadequate management, procurement problems, and difficulty with social issues.

Mainstreaming environmental concerns in policy reforms and in the public investment program should be an important focus of Bank efforts in India. This would include addressing environmental safeguards further upstream, supporting alternatives to public sector management of water supply and sewerage systems, promoting rational pricing of natural resources, backing enforcement efforts of the existing comprehensive environmental legislation, and expanding use of the Global Environment Facility to address greenhouse gas and ozone production and to reverse threats to biodiversity.

Health

The Bank health program is now on the right track, having improved considerably during the last decade. Its assistance program was built on the findings of *World Development Report 1993*, solid sector work conducted in collaboration with Indian expertise, effective policy dialogue, and recognition that there needed to be a focus on specific diseases. The result was a series of broad-based projects that focused on maternal and child care (also as a way to address population policy issues), on specific diseases, and on state-level health system reform. Comments from the Ministry of Health and Family Welfare express satisfaction with the Bank's contribution to physical capacity, but also note its modest past achievements in institutional development. The government's withdrawal from the Tamil Nadu nutrition model has been a big disappointment, but the Bank has continued to encourage the incorporation of successful aspects of that experience in the Integrated Child Development Services projects.

Four projects addressing specific diseases— leprosy, blindness, tuberculosis, and malaria— were included in the program, and two HIV/AIDS projects were added during the 1990s. The first of these, which closed in fiscal 1999, initiated significant nationwide HIV/AIDS prevention and awareness activities. The program has dramatically improved the blood supply and public knowledge of HIV and has increased condom use considerably in high-risk groups. Bank performance on the design and supervision of this complex project was rated highly satisfactory by

OED in its review of the project's implementation completion report.

Education

In the early 1990s the Bank overcame the line ministry's resistance to lending for education projects, which was mainly due to fear of interference by outsiders in sensitive curriculum matters. Initially, the Bank assisted in the vocational/technical education area, with four projects that have been recently and successfully completed. Since October 1993 seven District Primary Education projects (DPEPs) have been approved and are still ongoing for $1.2 billion in gross commitments from the Bank and with a large amount of parallel donor financing. These projects focused on increasing access to primary education for the disadvantaged, particularly children from scheduled tribes and castes and girls; capacity building; and quality improvement.

The large efforts to promote primary education have been accompanied by high government commitment, innovative thinking, and an emphasis on carrying out project preparation work with local staff only, who in the process learned a great deal. Overall about 50 million children have been involved, and large enrollment increases, especially of girls, have been reported in the most deprived areas.[4] Some questions have been raised among donors, scholars and nongovernmental organizations (NGOs), however, regarding the reliability of enrollment data, the extent of quality improvements, the functioning of the village education committees, and the tight control by the government of school visits and supervision reports.[5] This suggests a need for an independent verification.

Public Financial Accountability: A Promising Beginning

The risk of fraud, waste, and abuse of public funds has been growing in the past decades, partly fueled by the rapid economic growth that has benefited many in the private sector and by the increased availability of luxury goods. Public financial accountability is a recent area of emphasis for the Bank, whose knowledge of the issues in this area at the country and state levels is growing. That knowledge is centered on financial management and internal control procedures in the central government and, very recently, in a few focus states, especially Uttar Pradesh. But there are still significant gaps in knowledge—the most significant being the effectiveness of the legislative scrutiny processes at the center and at the states.

The Bank has not yet articulated a comprehensive long-term assistance strategy for strengthening public financial accountability in India. While elements of a strategy have been slowly emerging at the state level, the Bank has yet to deal with public financial accountability issues at the country level. At the project level the Bank has made efforts to improve accounting, auditing, and budgeting systems at the implementing agency level and in specific operating departments in state governments. Outside Uttar Pradesh, however, these interventions were not designed to address the significant capacity problems in the state or country's overall public financial accountability systems.

Regarding Bank-financed projects, lessons with implementing the Loans Administration Change Initiative suggest the importance of:

- Bank and borrower commitment to enhance financial management and control
- Training and experience of Bank staff in public sector auditing, accounting, and scrutiny systems
- Communication to the borrower of consequences for less-than-satisfactory compliance with fiduciary obligations as specified in the loan agreements.

With the recent emphasis on programmatic lending in India, the adequacy of the overall public financial accountability systems at the national and subnational level has assumed greater importance. The Bank has done pioneering work in this area in Uttar Pradesh, but this initiative alone may not be sufficient. Unless the Bank engages in a productive dialogue and partnership with the central government on the systematic modernization of public financial accountability systems in the country, its current efforts in a few focus states may be neither effective nor sustainable. The June 2000 Lucknow conference for speakers of state legislatures proved to be an ideal forum and first step for the Bank to articulate its views to a national audience on the need for improvements in this area.

Mainstreaming Participation, but Resettlement Safeguards Are Still Contentious

Social development received inadequate attention in Bank-assisted projects before the 1990s. Serious problems had accumulated, mainly caused by poor involuntary resettlement practices, which seriously damaged the reputations of India and the Bank (the Morse Commission's review in 1992 highlighted serious deficiencies on the part of the Bank) and forced remedial work. Much of this work, however, was concentrated on specific projects, with limited attention to systemic issues. Numerous projects were canceled, suspended, or restructured.[6] The Bank became reluctant to take on, and the government hesitant to seek Bank support for, projects with resettlement implications, such as large-scale irrigation, power generation, and road projects.

Recent Bank initiatives hold more promise, but to assess the longer-term results and sustainability of the steps taken so far, better monitoring and evaluation systems are needed. The emphasis has expanded from "do no harm" in social safeguard policies to a more proactive approach in the second half of the 1990s: improving Bank and borrower performance through social assessment, participatory approaches, decentralization, increased transparency and accountability, and community empowerment. During fiscal 1994–98, India had the second-highest percentage (81 percent) of Bank-assisted projects approved with community participation among all Bank borrowers with more than 10 projects. Each later project round has built on the lessons of previous efforts to achieve greater participation.[7] Social development issues have indeed become more integrated and mainstreamed in Bank operations. Although the government has made uneven progress in adopting participatory approaches, it is moving forward with Bank encouragement and assistance.

The application of the Bank's resettlement policy, however, remains contentious. In complaints raised by community organizations and NGOs about the National Thermal Power Corporation (NTPC) Power Generation project in 1997 and the Ecodevelopment project in 1998, an independent inspection panel found merit to the claims of project area residents and tribal people that they had been (or might be) harmed by involuntary resettlement and that their interests had been neglected. The Bank admitted policy violations regarding the involuntary resettlement complaint and implementation shortcomings regarding the peoples' interests. It adopted corrective action plans.

At the same time, the Bank is often seen as too rigid in applying its resettlement policy and too accommodating of NGO agendas. Some senior NTPC and government officials raised with OED missions the issue of the Bank's insistence on retroactive application of its resettlement policy to projects the Bank did not originally finance. The officials also raised the issue of differential treatment of resettled people in Bank-financed projects compared with other projects, some covering adjacent areas, where lower standards were applied. They expressed dissatisfaction with field office staff's lack of authority to make decisions based on local realities and with such issues being routinely referred to headquarters staff, who apply rigid interpretations of Bank guidelines on safeguards.

Despite the concerns of some officials, for the most part the government accepts and supports the Bank's approach. The Bank has indeed positively influenced the resettlement debate in India and its guidelines have become the de facto standard against which civil society measures government performance. During the 1990s, in an attempt to harmonize approaches, the Bank engaged in policy dialogue about the differences between Bank and other donor guidelines and Indian laws and practices. The major difference is that, while the Indian approach is limited to compensation for loss of land and other assets, Bank standards require that attention also be given to potential loss of livelihood for poor and vulnerable people. Thus, Bank-supported projects require a broader set of supportive measures for affected people. Such additional support, however, is complementary to, rather than in conflict with, Indian laws and practices.

Given the impasse at the center, the Bank focused on sector and state policies where it has had greater success. Sectoral resettlement policies in line with Bank safeguards have been adopted for the coal sector and for highways by the central government and a few state governments. Similarly, some states have adopted safeguards for all their public irrigation projects. The recently approved *National Highways III* project, with full attention to safeguards, and the central government's application of the Bank's approach to resettlement and social assessment to some other non-Bank financed road projects are strong evidence of commitment and ownership by at least some parts of the government.

Nevertheless, the high-level policy dialogue has been insufficient so far at the national and state levels. Drafts of a new national resettlement policy and proposed amendments to the Land Acquisition Act in line with Bank guidelines have been awaiting cabinet approval for the past five years. And the perception of unreasonableness among some senior officials regarding the Bank's application of its guidelines in central ministries and in the NTPC remains an area of concern.

Gender: Unsuccessful Mainstreaming

The Bank has not succeeded in mainstreaming gender issues across sectors. Attention to gender issues has been mainly confined to enclave activities in the social sectors. While Bank lending and nonlending operations in education and women's health have taken women's issues into account, the picture for operations in agriculture, basic health, water supply and sanitation, irrigation, rural finance, rural transport, and environment is disappointing. The failure is in implementation rather than conceptualization. The Bank's sector work in these areas recognized women's issues, and many project documents addressed gender concerns at entry. However, at implementation these concerns often take a back seat. Moreover, monitoring of gender disaggregated results of lending operations remains deficient. Finally, in such sectors as industry, energy, transport, and finance, there has been little or no recognition of gender issues.

5

THE DEVELOPMENT EFFECTIVENESS OF BANK ASSISTANCE

The Elusive Counterfactual

There are no easy ways to construct a counterfactual to the Bank's assistance efforts in a large country such as India, which was always more important to the Bank than vice versa (see Chapter 2). Without Bank support for adjustment in the early 1990s, would India have undertaken reforms and experienced the same acceleration of income growth and urban poverty reduction? The broad thrust of the reforms would likely have been carried out without the Bank on the strength of the high degree of country ownership and commitment, reinforced by the collapse of the Soviet Union (India's political ally) and its planned economy and by China's spectacular growth since it opened to the global economy. The Bank brought technical expertise, but Indian economists (inside and outside the country, in the public and private sectors) are world renowned for their analytical strength and could have provided similar advice.

If Bank management had been bolder in its public pronouncements on fiscal issues (as it was at the May 2000 Paris donors meeting) and had made fiscal balance a condition for the two adjustment operations that followed the first Structural Adjustment Credit/Structural Adjustment Loan and also for its overall lending volume, would the country have a smaller deficit today? Louder warnings might have better focused the internal political and academic debate on subsidy reduction and civil service downsizing. They might also have limited India's quick re-

turn to the international capital markets, strengthening the fiscal authorities' efforts to rein in spending pressures and raise tax collection against the background of a deep-rooted political opposition to such reforms.

If Bank assistance had been more focused on rural development and agricultural policy issues and rainfed agriculture since the early 1990s, would the country have achieved deeper reductions in rural poverty? Former Bank officials stress the difficulty of addressing these issues rather than lack of effort arising from diffuse and overlapping institutional responsibilities. Former senior government officials, moreover, believe that the government could not have opened another battlefront with critics of the reform program of the early 1990s and could not have weathered the political implications of sensitive reforms, such as the withdrawal of input subsidies from farmers. At a minimum, an earlier focus by the Bank on institutional reform, participation, and decentralization in project design, implementation, and monitoring and evaluation would have led to better project performance. Equally, widely disseminated sector work and an explicit sector assistance strategy might have helped the internal debate and accelerated high-level consideration of agricultural reform issues.

If the Bank had focused earlier and with more effort on analyzing sectorwide policy and institutional constraints, widely disseminated its conclusions beyond the small group of committed reformers in government with whom it worked closely, and withheld sectoral lending until satisfied with actions or commitments taken to overcome such constraints, it might have contributed to a faster pace of domestic reform. This is what happened in the power sector after the Bank refused to lend unless policies and institutions were reformed. With the benefit of hindsight, it can be seen that budgetary, agricultural, or social safety net reforms, for instance, could already have started (in the mid- or late-1990s), with a positive long-term impact on rural poverty.

Development Effectiveness: Improving

Relevance and Efficacy

Although the Bank neglected rural poverty in the first half of the 1990s, it provided timely support to structural adjustment for the resumption of economic growth, which was the most pressing priority. It also showed increased concern for the adequacy of the policy and institutional framework in the energy sector and gave much attention to human development.

The relevance of Bank assistance continued to be substantial in the second half of the 1990s, as its concern for the adequacy of the policy and

institutional framework expanded to other sectors (especially water resources) and to the states, and thanks to its in-depth study of India's rural development strategy and heightened attention in its lending program to social development and rural poverty. Relevance has improved further in the past three years, as the Bank has recognized the importance and urgency of comprehensive fiscal adjustment, sharpened and operationalized its state focus, and intensified its decentralized and participatory interventions.

The achievements of the Bank's strategic objectives in the 1990s are undeniable. Creditworthiness, stabilization, and faster growth on the heels of the fiscal and structural reforms of the early 1990s were already in hand by the mid-1990s. Some progress has also been made in more rational pricing and institutions for power and, to a limited extent, water. Social indicators have continued to improve. Urban poverty has declined. With the support of the Bank and other external partners, India's mindset is more open and relies more on markets and the private sector. From a closed and controlled economy, India has indeed moved far toward integration in the global economy.

However, macroeconomic stability has been at risk since 1997 because of the fiscal deficit. Economic growth has come down to between 5 to 6 percent beginning in 1997, partly as a result of the slowdown in the pace of structural reform, and partly due to the ripples in Indian export competitiveness from the East Asian crisis. Poverty reduction has been limited, with severe poverty in rural areas associated with inadequate social and infrastructural services. A large reform agenda still remains a decade after India broke away from the old development model.

All in all, the efficacy of the Bank's assistance is rated modest for both the first and second halves of the 1990s. For the decade overall, excellent results in power and good results in increasing competition, openness and the role of the private sector, health, and education must be balanced against modest impacts on rural and urban development, financial sector development, public sector management, environmental protection, and gender (see Chapter 4); the limited impact of economic and sector work; and the mediocre performance of completed projects. Efficiency has been adequate—somewhat behind other large countries but higher than for most countries.

It is still too early to gauge the efficacy of the most recent Country Assistance Strategy. Moreover, the sanctions imposed in the wake of nuclear testing undermined the implementation of key aspects of the 1997 assistance strategy. In particular, they blurred the link between the overall volume of lending and the country's macro and sectoral performance, infrastructure reforms, and the quality of its public investment.

Outcome

On balance, therefore, in light of *substantial* relevance but *modest* efficacy, this Country Assistance Evaluation finds the outcome of Bank country assistance moderately satisfactory for both the first and the second halves of the 1990s. However, the higher relevance and promising steps taken following the 1997 strategic shift in Bank assistance promise better efficacy and, thus, presage a satisfactory outcome for current Bank efforts, provided India intensifies its reform efforts.

Institutional Development Impact

The institutional development impact of past Bank assistance is modest, although here again the Bank's recent attention to governance issues (as in Uttar Pradesh); its heightened link of lending to overall policy and institutional performance; and the mainstreaming of participation in project design, implementation, and monitoring presage a substantial impact ahead.

Sustainability

Broader appreciation of the need for continuing reforms and the fruits of increased interstate competition for private investment and economic and social progress suggest further progress ahead. But the economy remains vulnerable to macroeconomic shocks, which may cause reversal of structural reforms. The economy's ability to sustain investment and current growth rates and to further reduce poverty is threatened by the continuing large fiscal imbalances and new military spending pressures, environmental damage, populist approaches to subsidies and trade, and poor governance. Hence

the sustainability of the benefits from past and ongoing Bank assistance remains uncertain.

Bank and Borrower Performance: Mixed

Exogenous Factors

As the global environment remained favorable overall throughout the 1990s, with only a slight deterioration between mid-1997 and the end of 1998 due to the impact of the East Asian crisis on Indian export competitiveness and foreign investment, the contribution of exogenous factors to the achievement of Bank objectives was positive.

Bank Performance

Bank performance in the design and delivery of its assistance has greatly improved since the 1980s, while ensuring borrower ownership. Increasingly during the 1990s the Bank:

- Supported important reforms initiated by the center and some states with timely and well-regarded analyses, advice, and creative lending instruments
- Withheld or reduced lending to some agencies and states reluctant to embrace necessary reforms (for example, in power), even at the cost of painful negative consequences for its lending volume and staff job security
- Greatly expanded its assistance in the social sectors, critical to its long-term mission of poverty reduction
- Recognized the increasing importance of the states, adjusted its assistance accordingly, and focused on those interested in reform
- Devoted more resources and management attention to improving participation
- Improved portfolio performance
- Embarked on a deep (and ongoing) review of its sectoral assistance strategies (in urban and rural development and in water resource management) where development results had been unsatisfactory.

But the Bank did not:

- Pay enough attention (until recently) to inadequate agricultural policies and stagnating rural poverty (the slow-down in agricultural wages should have been enough of a warning bell, even before poverty estimates became available)

- Sufficiently emphasize the need for public sector management and judicial reforms in its economic and sector work and policy dialogue
- Improve the reach and impact of its economic and sector work
- Broaden the aim of its project assistance to achieve sectoral policy or institutional reform objectives
- Mainstream gender across all sectors in a country with a high gender gap
- Track the gender and poverty-reduction impacts of its own projects
- Withhold financial assistance to sectors with inadequate commitment to reform (agriculture and banking).

Borrower Performance

The central government's core economic ministries initiated and sustained several very important reforms that substantially opened the private sector to internal and external competition. The ministries pushed for expanding Bank assistance in the social sectors to increase the absorption of available external funds for development and supported the Bank's firm stance on power reform and its recent direct policy dialogue with the states. The committed leadership of a handful of states seized the opportunities for strengthening their development strategies offered by the Bank's eager search for new channels to support policy and institutional reforms.

At the same time, Indian authorities failed to resolve the fiscal deficit problem; to shift spending toward operations and maintenance, infrastructure investment, and the social sectors; to accelerate the pace of structural reforms and extend them to agriculture; to design a more pro-poor rural development strategy; and to address adequately governance and environmental problems. Indian authorities must share responsibility with the Bank for the slow disbursement of Bank loans and credits and the mediocre outcome and institutional development impact of the overall portfolio.

6

IMPROVING ASSISTANCE FOR HIGHER REACH AND IMPACT

With more than a quarter (more than 300 million) of the world's poor, India's performance is critical to achieving the International Development Goals, which include halving poverty worldwide by 2015.[1] As India has become more open to the world economy, it has also become more receptive to external contributions to its development policies. The Bank's capacity and credibility remain high and its new emphasis on knowledge transfer is welcome in India. Resource transfer, however, remains critical to the Bank's capacity to engage the Indian authorities in a dialogue about policy and institutional reforms and to influence their design and implementation. In such an environment the comparative advantage of the Bank lies in the combination of money and knowledge transfer—that is, policy and technical analyses and advice—targeted to high-impact development issues.

In the past three years the Bank has moved in the right direction and has been more selective than it was earlier in the 1990s in its lending and nonlending services. The five pillars and the fiscal and structural reform triggers of the 1997 Country Assistance Strategy remain valid. Thus, except for adjustments to accelerate and assure the full application of those pillars and triggers, no substantive changes in the assistance strategy appear necessary.

Lending Instruments

The Bank should scale up and direct new lending assistance only to those sectors where central and state governments exhibit strong ownership of policy and institutional reform programs, as it has successfully done in the energy sector. Adaptable program loans are appropriate instruments to support sectorwide public investments when there is commitment to an adequate policy and institutional framework, but the future pace of progress is also less than certain. Program or adjustment quick-disbursing lending is also appropriate for supporting statewide comprehensive reform efforts. As seen in Uttar Pradesh, a planned series of single tranche operations rewarding the adoption of concrete actions taken before presentation to the board of directors is preferable to multiyear, condition-laden operations, in light of the country's sensitivity to external interference.

Lending Linkage

The Bank should link overall lending volumes to progress in structural reforms in agriculture and implementation of an effective rural development strategy, as progress in these areas is crucial for rural poverty reduction. This would be in addition to maintaining the current link between the overall lending volume and fiscal discipline and between sectoral lending volumes and sector-specific policy and institutional frameworks or reform programs. The Bank already has an internal management system for country performance scoring, but its component weights and the quality, transparency, and comprehensiveness of the criteria used need adaptation to India's circumstances in consultation with government and civil society. The Bank's most recent economic report is a good basis for such consultations.

State Focus

Given the states' important responsibilities in infrastructure and social services, their greater autonomy from the central government, and their diversity in institutional, policy, human, and social capabilities, an intensified state focus by the Bank is appropriate. The Bank should concentrate new lending in reforming states, where it has agreed on an assistance strategy with governments (as piloted in Uttar Pradesh).[2] In nonreforming states, assistance should be limited to policy dialogue, clarification of performance criteria, economic and sector work to contribute to the internal debate (including work through reputable Indian institutes), and pilot projects that can demonstrate the benefits of policy and institutional reforms. In parallel the Bank should assist the government (and relevant committees) in introducing performance-based allocations of central government and external resources to the states.

Program Priorities

The priority areas of engagement for India's external development partners mirror the large, un-

finished reform agenda for poverty reduction described in Chapter 1. Specific sectoral priorities for Bank assistance, however, should emerge from a renewed dialogue and an explicit division of responsibilities among the Bank, government, civil society, and development partners.

There is an urgent need to reduce macroeconomic vulnerability and public deficits (through reductions in subsidies, public employment, public enterprise losses, and tax reforms) and to increase economic efficiency, international competitiveness, and the labor intensity of growth (through trade liberalization, privatization, labor market reform, and judicial reform). The Bank should continue to cover these areas with policy analyses (such as those relevant for India in World Trade Organization negotiations) and economic and sector work. And it should offer lending support for easing the pain of labor dislocations to accelerate the pace of reform, especially of the government's divestment plans.

There is also an urgent need for the Bank to scale up assistance for capacity building in public financial accountability from the project to national and subnational levels. The Bank should augment its skill base in project financial management with specialists in public accountability systems.

In power, transport, urban development (especially in the area of safe and adequate water supplies and sanitation facilities), and the environment, the Bank's experience in India and around the world, the large gap between needs and available resources, and the scope for pricing, regulatory, and other policy and institutional reforms (say, for water and power) justify the Bank's continuing involvement. Bank assistance should help maximize private sector participation and competition in these areas through guarantees, appropriate incentives for good management of public agencies, and strengthening of capacity for enforcing environmental regulations and safeguards.

For rural development, especially in rainfed areas, the Bank should support policy reforms in agriculture, capacity building at the district and village levels, and enhanced community participation in project planning, implementation, maintenance, and evaluation (as through projects of the District Poverty Initiative type). And the Bank should help expand public investment for rural infrastructure, agricultural technology, and sustainable forestry.

In health, the Bank should continue its dual focus on nationwide diseases (including HIV infections) and statewide institutional reforms. In future assistance to education, the Bank should focus on poor people's access to basic education in all districts of the country, rather than only in District Primary Education project districts; improved availability of teachers; and higher quality of instruction. It should also recommend an independent impact evaluation and verification of the flow of funds to the beneficiaries at the local level, an integrated study of and assistance approach to education subsectors, direct lending to states, and a better use of international technical expertise.

Analytical Work

To maximize the impact of economic and sector work on policy analysts and decisionmakers, the Bank should intensify its partnerships with Indian research and policy institutes and focus on relevant international experiences and cost-benefit analyses of policy options. A new public expenditure review focused on incidence analysis would be an important tool for the Bank in providing policy advice on reform of social safety net programs and on the restructuring of public expenditures. The Bank should also ensure wide dissemination among stakeholders and the general public, preferably through government agencies or local think tanks. Conclusions from economic and sector work should be drawn more sharply, but detailed proposals should continue to be discussed confidentially with government officials.

Monitoring

Although the Bank's assistance has become more pro-poor, the Bank should systematically monitor the poverty and gender impacts of Bank-assisted projects and programs. It should also help government agencies do the same for their public expenditure programs. Given the large gender gap the Bank should also make greater

efforts to mainstream gender beyond the social sectors.

Participation

The Bank should continue to foster participatory institutions and to assist Indian ownership and capacity for comprehensive social development. A balanced approach needs to be pursued that focuses on implementation as much as preparation. It should also give the same weight to understanding and improving incentive structures of the institutions responsible for social development programs as to prescriptive rules.

Safeguards

Bank management should, as a matter of priority, clarify with the government and other donors the mandatory nature, rationale, and scope of the safeguard standards to be applied in Bank-supported projects, especially for resettlement. To help engender gradual improvements in India's standards, the Bank should engage "focus state" governments in a dialogue on such standards as part of its discussions about reforms and policy-based lending.

Aid Coordination

To foster client leadership and ownership in aid coordination, the Bank should continue to endorse government preparation and direction of formal aid coordination meetings and provide logistical support as required. At such meetings, the Bank should also continue to present a transparent and candid scorecard of country development performance, as it did in 2000. To enhance the effectiveness of external assistance and partnerships and to enable greater selectivity in its own assistance, the Bank should strengthen informal, in-country donor coordination on Country Assistance Strategies and on critical sector strategies where consultations among donor and development agencies have been lacking (for example, agriculture and rural development). The Bank should also endeavor to reverse the decline in cofinancing for its operations, seek out donors' expertise more systematically, and encourage other agencies to take the lead in external assistance in their areas of strength.

The Bank's Efficiency

Finally, the Bank should analyze sources and justifications for the higher budgetary costs for project preparation (to Board approval) for India than for other large countries. It may consider shifting more project preparation responsibilities to the client.

THE CLIENT'S EVALUATION OF BANK ASSISTANCE

Given India's importance to the Bank, extensive exit consultations on the India Country Assistance Evaluation (CAE) took place from March 14 to April 7, 2000, including a series of workshops. These were organized jointly with the South Asia Region, which took the opportunity for beginning consultations on the next Country Assistance Strategy (CAS).[1]

Civil Society's Views from the CAE/CAS Synthesis Workshop

In general, the series of workshops was much appreciated by Indian stakeholders, as they showed the face of a new Bank willing to confront frankly and openly its past weaknesses and interested in the suggestions of a broader audience on its future assistance program. All the voices heard, even when critical of the Bank, wanted more and better involvement by the Bank rather than less. Summary minutes of the sectoral workshops can be found in annexes to their respective CAE background papers (see Bibliography). The following is a summary of the views expressed by discussants and participants at the CAE/CAS synthesis workshop on April 6, 2000.

The panel discussants stressed some of the themes in the CAE, including:

- The need to help restore fiscal health at the center and in the states
- Long-standing poor performance by the Bank in institutional development (for example, with technical assistance and the railways, with urban development, and in support of the country's decentralization)
- The Bank's lack of attention to public sector management
- The centrality of rural development to poverty reduction and the need for the Bank to address it
- The limited access to and dissemination of economic and sector work
- The desirability of involvement of policy researchers around the country in economic and sector work
- The need for the Bank to mainstream gender concerns and to form real partnerships at the local level to go beyond the token partnerships
- The need to improve project implementation performance
- The wisdom of continuing to support power sector reforms.

A discussant challenged the CAE's endorsement of the shift in Bank assistance strategy toward the "reforming states," cautioning that the states least likely to succeed are the ones trying hardest to lure the Bank. The same discussant also challenged the Bank's shift toward soft sectors and soft issues, and stressed the need for long-term capital financing of infrastructure projects (irrigation, urban development, transport, and power). The discussant also challenged the Bank's comparative advantage to support the policy and institutional reform requirements, as well as the financing, of such investments.

Another discussant thought that OED had overplayed the influence of the Bank on policy (see the counterfactual questions in Chapter 5) regarding the reforms of the early 1990s and the fiscal deficit, and challenged the OED view that the Bank was at fault for not emphasizing agricultural reform issues in its policy dialogue during the early and mid-1990s. The Bank was criticized for its "zeal for participation," which often leads it to set up organizations that parallel existing ones (that is, the *Panchayats*).

The discussants also suggested new (but sometimes conflicting) priorities for future assistance. These included capacity building for existing institutions at the local level; vocational education and technical training for industry and the health sector; focus assistance on the 125 poorest districts, in addition to the reforming states; close collaboration with the Planning Commission on common development and poverty reduction strategies; investment in power generation (which the Bank had avoided during the late 1990s); and investment in social sectors, which a participant saw as the only justifiable area for Bank financing given India's easy access to international capital markets for infrastructure projects.

In the open discussion that followed, the high quality and positive impact of the Bank's work was recognized ("The Bank has been a consistent force for the past decades for integrating India in the world economy, which today is an unqualified success"). Most participants agreed on the need to work with states, given their increased autonomy from the center and their primary responsibilities in health, education, water, power, and the like; on the need to reach beyond the "focus" states of assistance; and on the necessity and desirability of the Bank's recommended agenda of structural reforms. But beyond this, two strands of comments emerged.

Academic and government officials supported the Bank focus on power sector reforms, and also mentioned the need to expand Bank assistance to the urban transport sector. Some noted a sense of dispersion of Bank efforts and resources and wished it would concentrate its human and financial resources on infrastructure. But many expressed reservations about the strategies for focus states of the Bank and other development agencies because the strategies implied neglect of the needs (including advice) of states deemed "not sufficiently reforming." There was also concern expressed that the criteria for the Bank's definition of "reforming states" are not transparent, because the analytical and reform work in the reforming states is not being adequately disseminated to other states, and that states that are reforming may not like to be channeled to only one international donor or lender. Academic and government officials also expressed deep concerns about the effect of a strict application of the Bank's environmental and resettlement safeguards, the latter being seen as creating islands of affluence with respect to government-supported or other donor-supported programs.

Other participants, mainly representatives of nongovernmental organizations (NGOs), cautioned that power should not dominate the Bank assistance agenda and that there is a need to keep a balance with other sectors. They expressed a preference for less selectivity and more holistic approaches. The participants stressed the need for the Bank to pay close attention to the poor (endorsing the idea of a focus on the 125 poorest districts) above growth and, regardless of the choice of reforming states, to make better use of local partnerships and to pay more attention to the social dimensions of the structural reforms and to the environment. For instance, one of the participants mentioned that the Bank's focus on specific diseases (malaria, HIV/AIDS) overlooks other serious diseases, such as diarrhea.

Feedback from the India-Based CAE Advisers

Reflecting on the main messages from the synthesis workshop, the India-based CAE advisers stressed:[2]
- The high payoff of better dissemination of economic and sector work

- The importance of the Bank's long term lending role
- The centrality of the fiscal/power sector crisis and of fiscal discipline for both central and state governments
- The need for the Bank to remain engaged with the central government and not put all its eggs in reforming states' baskets
- The need to be honest about the fiscal health of reforming states
- The need to help capacity building at the *Panchayat* level
- The need to focus on a few areas of assistance where a critical mass of expertise is built up over time and then maintained (unlike in urban development).

One of the advisers remarked that the current lending mix (a third social, a third rural, a third infrastructure) is about right and that the Bank cannot deal only with fiscal/power issues, as it has done in recent years. Others stressed that lending ought to consider the Bank's comparative advantage in infrastructure (especially by helping public institutions build public-private partnerships, as in housing finance or through support to the Industrial Credit and Investment Corporation of India) and focus on the lack of an adequate policy and institutional framework in agriculture. Another adviser thought that the CAE draft needed a better distillation of generic lessons from successes and failures and a sharper discussion of the Bank's comparative advantage. Finally, the neglect by the 1997 CAS of trade issues was noted, with the implication that the CAE should give trade more emphasis than the January 31 draft did. On the delicate question of the Bank's policy influence, advisers sided with the camp that thinks the Bank succeeded only in those areas where India had decided to go on its own and that there are no known instances where the Bank's influence caused, rather than supported, a policy shift.

On the CAE draft in particular, the advisers thought the tone was right—balanced and frank—and that the open discussion process had been—and will be—much appreciated. The concluding chapter (Chapter 6 in the current version) needed a better reflection of the controversy heard over alternative directions for Bank assistance.

In conclusion, the key ingredients for effectiveness for the Bank in India were identified as focusing on key areas ahead of time and staying with them over the long term; widespread dissemination of analysis and recommendations; providing support at the right time; and bringing international experience to bear.

Feedback from the Government

During the April 2000 exit consultations in New Delhi, the OED mission held meetings on an earlier version of the CAE (a draft dated January 31, 2000) with officials of the Ministry of Finance and the Planning Commission, senior economic advisers to the government and the main opposition party, a former minister of finance in the early 1990s, and the former counterpart in the Ministry of Finance (until end-1999) of the Bank country director.

OED's interpretation of the rural poverty trends (amended in the current CAE draft to better reflect the controversy over poverty estimates) and its criticism of the Bank for not paying more attention to agricultural and rural development policy issues (still standing in the current CAE draft) were challenged by some within this group. But otherwise no other major concerns or differences were raised with the substance and tone of the evaluation.

Government officials were supportive of the Bank's new approach of focusing on reforming states, which in their view had been quite effective in nudging states to move forward. But they would like the Bank to be more proactive in talking to nonreforming states and to support some islands of excellence in those states as well (note, however, that the Ministry of Human Resource Development had reservations on this point). Well aware of the risk of macroeconomic instability, government officials also believe that fiscal pressures need to be dealt with both at the center and the state levels. In fact, were the focus exclusively on the states, some of them would try to pass on their fiscal problems to the federal government.

To reduce poverty, the priority reforms should be to address agricultural policies and reduce the anti-labor and anti-export bias of the current industrial regulations. Diversified agriculture must be a focal area of assistance, more so than irrigated agriculture.

In resource transfer, the Bank may not be large, but it brings standards, learning, and discipline. These byproducts are very valuable. Even from a strict financial standpoint, the Bank's contribution is not trivial, as long-term sources of financing are still limited for India in both the domestic and international capital markets. As for the actual lending volume, it was not the government's decision to borrow only $1.1 billion in fiscal 1999, as it was and still is eager to borrow more in the $2.4–3 billion range. The quality of current financial auditing work is high. The Bank and government do not need any other parallel auditing system.

Other officials, however, stressed that Bank financing is paltry compared with total public expenditures and that it would be more productive for the Bank to focus on improving the quality of public expenditures. Given the shrinking (absolute and relative) size of Bank lending to India, the Bank role should be catalytic and innovative. The dual goals of Bank assistance should be growth and equality of opportunity. Because agricultural liberalization may well have an adverse effect in the short term on rural welfare, unless the employment effect is very strong, the Bank may be needed to help cushion the blow. Other priorities should be in infrastructure, social sectors, quality of education, ways to support the first student in a family to attend school, and capacity building, especially at the *Panchayat* level.

Officials noted that monitoring and evaluation is one of the weakest areas in the country, and an area where the Bank should help. They stressed the need for easy dissemination of economic and sector work, especially on the Internet. Economic and sector work can be subcontracted to local institutions, but India still has much to learn from the Bank's knowledge of international experience and best practices. Officials stressed that the Bank's economic and sector work has been "extremely helpful in policy formulation and its implementation." For instance, the value in the most recent Bank economic report is that it stimulates thinking and debate about important issues, without committing the government to any specific point of view or suggestion.

Some officials expressed concern at the length of the Bank's project preparation cycle (two years, with the third Madras Water Supply project under preparation for seven years). Learning and innovation loans from the Bank are not worth the trouble for the government, as there is too little money involved. Shifting goalposts during project preparation is a problem (for example, the Bank is making the Tamil Nadu desalinization plant shut down before the Bank will give assistance).

While government officials agree in principle on the thrust of the Bank's resettlement safeguards, various officials argued that the Bank was often blind in its interpretation. ("In one case, Bank staff even insisted on a specific room size. If India were to adopt and publicize the Bank's position on squatters' right, it would make it impossible to acquire more land for public projects.")

In addition to the feedback recorded above on the January 31, 2000, draft, the government also had the opportunity to comment on the October 24, 2000, draft, which already reflected feedback from the government and the South Asia Region. With respect to the October 24, 2000, CAE draft, only the Ministry of Human Resource Development provided comments.

ANNEXES

ANNEX A: REFERENCE TABLES

Table A.1: Economic and Social Indicators for India and Selected Comparators

A. PEOPLE AND QUALITY OF LIFE	India 1986-90	India 1991-93	India 1994-97	India 1998	India 1999	Pakistan 1994-99	Sri Lanka 1994-99	China 1994-99	Low income 1994-99
Population and labor force									
Land area (000's sq km.)	2,973	2,973	2,973	..	..	771	65	9,326	30,175
Population, total (million)	850	898	961	980	998	135	19	1,250	2,417
Population growth (%)	2.1	1.9	1.7	1.8	1.8	2.4	1.1	0.9	1.9
Population density, rural (people per sq km)	388	407	410	..	..	388	1,601	675	487
Labor force, total (million)	361	384	416	431	439	50	8	750	1,085
Labor force growth (growth rate %)	-0.3	1.8	4.1	1.8		2.4	1.2	0.9	1.7
Labor force, female (% of total)	31.4	31.5	31.9	32.1		27.7	36.2	45.2	40.6
Size of the economy									
GDP at market prices (current US $ b)	323	280	421	430	460	60	16	991	1,067
GNP at market prices (current US$ b)	319	276	417	426	446	61	15	975	1,838
GNP rank (percentile)	95th	96th	95th	95th	94th	100th	100th	89th	78th
GNP per capita, Atlas method (current US$)	400	330	430	440	450	470	820	780	410
GNP per capita Atlas method (growth, %)	3.5	3.1	3.2	4.3	4.9	1.2	2.7	6.3	2.5
GNP per capita rank (percentile)	99th	100th	100th	100th	100th	99th	99th	99th	99th
GNP per capita, PPP (current international $)	1,365	1,570	2,019	2,060	2,149	1,757	3,056	3,291	1,790
GNP per capita, PPP rank (percentile)	97th	97th	96th	96th	92nd	97th	94th	93rd	96th
Private consumption (annual % growth)	3.8	4.7	3.9	11.9	5.9	5.1	7.2	17.5	5.8
Poverty and inequality (%)									
Population below national poverty line (headcount)	34.1	40.9	35.0	..	..	34.0	35.3	6.0	..
Rural	34.3	43.5	36.7	..	..	36.9	38.1	7.9	..
Urban	33.4	33.7	30.5	..	..	28.0	28.4	1.9	..
Population below US$1 a day (headcount)	..	52.5	47.0	..	..	11.6	4.0	22.2	..
Poverty gap at US$1 a day	..	15.6	12.9	..	..	2.6	0.7	6.9	..
Population below US$2 a day (headcount)	..	88.8	87.5	..	..	57.0	41.2	57.8	..
Poverty gap at US$2 a day	..	45.8	42.9	..	..	18.6	11.0	24.1	..
Labor force, children 10-14 (% of age group)	16.7	..	13.5	..	..	16.8	2.3	10.1	20.8
GINI coefficient	..	33.8	29.7	..	..	31.2	30.1	41.5	..
Percentage share, lowest 10%	..	3.7	4.1	..	..	4.1	3.8	2.2	..
Percentage share, lowest 20%	8.8	8.5	9.2	..	..	7.4	8.9	5.5	..
Percentage share, highest 20%	41.3	42.6	39.3	..	..	41.2	39.3	47.5	..
Education									
Illiteracy rate, adult total (% of people 15+)	51.8	..	46.0	44.3	43.5	55.0	8.6	16.5	38.5
Illiteracy rate, adult male (% of males 15+)	38.2	..	33.3	32.9	32.2	41.1	5.7	8.8	29.1
Illiteracy rate, adult female (% of females 15+)	66.3	..	60.0	56.5	55.5	70.0	11.4	24.5	48.0
School enrollment, primary (% gross)	97.0	101.0	101.0	..	..	74.0	109.0	120.0	93.1
School enrollment, primary, female (% gross)	84.0	90.0	90.0	..	..	..	108.0	120.0	82.3
School enrollment, primary, male (% gross)	110.0	112.0	109.0	..	..	..	110.0	120.0	101.4
School enrollment, secondary (% gross)	44.0	49.0	49.0	..	..	..	75.0	70.0	41.9
School enrollment, secondary, male (% gross)	55.0	59.0	59.0	..	..	..	83.0	93.0	49.6
School enrollment, secondary, female (% gross)	33.0	38.0	39.0	..	..	..	83.0	94.0	33.2
Expected years of schooling gender gap (M-F)	..	..	..	..	..	..	..	..	..
Public expenditure on education (% of GNP)	..	..	3.4	..	..	3.0	3.4	2.3	..
Health									
Life expectancy at birth, total (years)	59.8	61.0	63.1	63.1	..	62.4	73.3	69.9	63.1
Life expectancy at birth, female (years)	60.0	62.0	64.0	63.9	..	63.3	75.6	71.5	64.3
Life expectancy at birth, male (years)	59.0	61.0	62.0	62.4	..	61.5	71.1	68.3	61.9
Safe water (% of population with access)	54.0	..	81.0	..	..	62.0	65.0	..	..
Safe water, rural (% of rural pop. with access)	47.0	..	79.0	..	..	56.0	88.0	..	..
Safe water, urban (% of urban pop. with access)	80.0	..	85.0	..	..	85.0	..	..	..
Sanitation (% of population with access)	14.0	..	29.0	..	..	39.0	..	..	..
Sanitation, urban (% of urban pop. with access)	44.0	..	70.0	..	..	75.0	..	..	..
Mortality rate, infant (per 1,000 live births)	83.4	74.0	62.9	69.8	..	91.5	16.4	31.1	67.6
Mortality rate, under-5 (per 1,000 live births)	110.0	..	..	83.0	..	120.0	18.0	36.0	92.1
Malnutrition prevalence (% of children under 5)	..	..	..	..	..	..	..	..	..
Contraceptive prevalence (% of women 15-49)	..	43.0	..	..	..	..	..	..	20.0
Fertility rate, total (births per woman)	3.7	3.4	3.1	3.2	..	4.9	2.1	1.9	3.1
Mortality ratio, maternal (per 100,000 live births)	..	437.0	440.0	..	..	..	30.0	115.0	702.8
Health expenditure, public (% of GDP)	1.3	0.8	0.7	..	..	0.9	1.4	2.1	1.0

Note: Latest single year when available. $ = US dollar.

Source: World Development Indicators (World Bank, 1999), Heritage Foundation, *World Competitiveness Yearbook* (1997), *International Country Risk Guide, Comprehensive Development Review* (6/30/99).

Table A.1: Economic and Social Indicators for India and Selected Comparators (continued)

	India	India	India	India	India	Pakistan	Sri Lanka	China	Low income
B. ENVIRONMENT, PHYSICAL INFRASTRUCTURE AND KNOWLEDGE	1986-90	1991-93	1994-97	1998	1999	1994-99	1994-99	1994-99	1994-99
Land use and agricultural productivity									
Land use, perm. cropland (% of land area)	2.1	2.4	2.4	..	..	0.7	15.5	1.2	12.0
Irrigated land (% of crop land)	26.6	29.5	33.6	..	..	81.0	29.2	37.0	24.2
Arable land (hectares per person)	0.20	0.18	0.17	..	..	0.17	0.05	0.10	0.19
Value added per hec. of agricultural land (1987 US$)	417.7	448.2	471.2	..	..	..	1,118.7	256.4	..
Agriculture value added / worker (1987 US$).	327.0	334.8	343.0	419.7	..	624.1	735.9	316.9	346.2
Food production index (1989-91 = 100)	99.9	108.8	118.5	119.7	123.3	141.4	114.3	158.8	128.2
Water use, deforestation, and protected areas				..					
Freshwater resources (cubic meters per capita)	..	..	2,167	1,947	..	1,938	2,329	2,285	4,330
Annual freshwater withdrawals	..	..		..	..	..	..	..	..
Level (billion cubic meters)	..	..	380.0	..	..	155.6	6.3	460.0	..
% of total resources	..	..	18.2	..	..	37.2	14.6	16.4	..
% for agriculture	..	..	93.0	..	..	97.0	96.0	87.0	90.0
% for industry	..	..	4.0	..	..	2.0	2.0	7.0	5.0
% for domestic use	..	..	3.0	..	..	2.0	2.0	6.0	5.0
Annual deforestation	..	..							
Square kilometers	..	..	650.0	..	..	0.8	0.3	8.8	65.5
Average annual % change	0.6	..	-0.01	..	..	3.4	1.4	0.7	0.8
Nationally protected areas									
Thousand square kilometers	..	..	142.9	..	..	37.2	8.6	598.1	1,650.0
% of total land area	..	..	4.8	..	..	4.8	13.3	6.4	5.5
Energy use and emissions									
Commercial energy use (kg of oil eqv. per capita)	423.6	442.9	476.2	..	..	445.8	371.2	902.4	461.0
Commercial energy use (kt of oil equivalent)	359,846	397,853	450,287	..	..	55,902	6,792	1,096,800	837,277
Commercial energy use, avg. annual growth (%)	1.6	1.0	1.3	..	..	2.1	3.0	3.8	1.2
GDP per unit of energy use (1987 US$ per kg of oil equiv.)	0.7	0.7	0.8	..	..	1.1	2.0	0.7	..
Energy imports, net (% of commercial energy use)	7.3	10.1	13.3	..	..	25.7	38.1	-0.3	-9.2
Electric power consumption (kwh per capita)	253.6	300.8	346.6	..	..	332.8	203.0	686.8	278.5
Electric power trans. and dist. loss (% of output)	18.2	16.8	18.0	..	..	23.1	17.0	7.1	19.3
CO_2 emissions, industrial (metric tons per capita)	0.8	0.9	1.1	..	..	0.8	0.4	2.7	0.7
CO_2 emissions, industrial (kt, thousands)	675.3	804.3	997.4	..	..	94.3	7.1	3,363.5	1,448.1
CO_2 emissions, industrial (kg per 1987 $ of GDP)	2.6	2.8	2.8	..	..	1.5	0.5	4.4	2.1
Transportation									
Roads, paved (%)	..	47.2	45.7	..	..	57.0	95.0	..	18.7
Roads, goods transported (million ton-km)	..	..	..	..	..	..	3,020	1,360,000	..
Railways, goods transported (ton-km per PPP $m. of GDP)	247,773	217,846	176,994	..	..	26,598	..	304,775	..
Air transport, passengers carried (thousands)	10,862	9,442	13,995	16,521	..	5,414	1,212	53,234	104,082
Communications, information, science, and technology									
Daily newspapers (per 1,000 people)	27.0	..	..	..	..	21.0	29.0	..	..
Radios (per 1,000 people)	79	80	105	..	..	92	210	195	117
Television sets (per 1,000 people)	31.9	50.1	69.1	..	..	87.9	92.0	269.0	57.3
Telephone mainlines (per 1,000 people)	5.9	8.9	18.6	22.0	..	19.4	28.4	69.6	36.8
Telephone ave. cost of local call (US$ per 3 min.s)	0.04	..	0.02	..	..	0.1	0.04	0.01	0.1
Mobile phones (per 1,000 people)	..	..	0.9	1.2	..	1.4	9.4	19.0	7.9
Personal computers (per 1,000 people)	0.3	0.6	2.1	2.7	..	3.9	4.1	8.9	6.2
Internet hosts (per 10,000 people)	..	..	0.1	0.1	0.1	0.2	0.3	0.1	0.3
Scientists and engineers in R&D (per million)	..	..	149	..	..	..	173	..	..
High-tech. exports (% of manufactured exp.s)	9.0	8.2	10.9	..	..	0.1	..	14.5	12.6
Number of patent applications filed by residents	..	..	6,632	..	..	16	50	11,698	..
Number of patent applications filed by nonresidents	..	..	1,660	..	..	782	21,138	41,016	..

Note: Latest single year when available. $ = US dollar.

Source: World Development Indicators (World Bank, 1999), Heritage Foundation, *World Competitiveness Yearbook* (1997), *International Country Risk Guide*.

Table A.1: Economic and Social Indicators for India and Selected Comparators (continued)

C. ECONOMY	India 1986-90	India 1991-93	India 1994-97	India 1998	India 1999	Pakistan 1994-99	Sri Lanka 1994-99	China 1994-99	Low income 1994-99
Growth of the economy (avg. annual, %)									
GDP growth (annual %)	6.6	3.7	7.0	6.1	6.2	3.9	4.7	7.1	3.6
Inflation, GDP deflator (annual %)	8.4	10.6	7.5	8.9	5.5	7.8	8.8	-1.1	..
Agriculture, value added (annual % growth)	4.7	2.8	2.0	7.6	3.0	0.4	2.5	2.8	
Industry, value added (annual % growth)	8.2	3.2	8.9	4.0	7.5	3.8	5.8	8.1	4.2
Services, etc., value added (annual % growth)	7.1	6.0	8.9	6.3	6.9	4.1	4.9	7.5	3.6
Exports of goods and services (annual % growth)	9.2	10.3	14.7	4.2	4.2	-1.2	1.0	7.9	6.1
Imports of goods and services (annual % growth)	4.9	5.8	8.2	12.0	5.5	-8.2	11.5	18.0	2.4
Structure of output									
Agriculture, value added (% of GDP)	31.0	30.5	25.0	29.3	28.5	25.9	21.1	17.3	23.0
Industry, value added (% of GDP)	29.3	27.8	30.0	24.7	25.1	25.4	27.5	49.7	38.9
Manufacturing, value added (% of GDP)	18.7	17.4	19.0	16.0	15.9	16.8	16.5	24.4	27.3
Services, etc., value added (% of GDP)	39.7	41.6	44.0	45.9	46.4	48.7	51.4	32.9	38.1
Structure of demand (% of GDP)									
Exports of goods and services (% of GDP)	7.7	10.8	11.5	11.0	10.7	14.9	36.0	21.8	23.7
Imports of goods and services (% of GDP)	10.6	12.2	15.5	13.8	14.2	19.2	42.4	19.9	22.1
Domestic absorption (% of GDP)	102.8	101.4	103.9	102.7	103.5	104.3	106.5	98.1	104.8
Private consumption, etc. (% of GDP)	66.1	68.6	70.0	68.6	69.0	78.3	71.3	49.7	58.9
General government consumption (% of GDP)	11.5	11.1	10.0	10.5	10.5	11.2	9.8	8.5	10.6
Gross domestic investment as % of GDP	23.2	21.3	24.0	23.6		17.1	25.4	38.3	28.9
Gross domestic fixed investment (% of GDP)	22.5	..	23.1	22.7	23.1	13.3	25.3	36.7	..
Public	..	..	..	..	..	..	..	..	..
Private	..	..	..	..	..	..	..	..	..
Gross domestic savings (% of GDP)	22.4	20.3	20.0	20.9	20.5	10.5	18.9	41.8	30.4
Gross national savings, including NCTR (% of GDP)	21.7	20.7	22.4	22.4	19.7	16.2	23.5	41.3	29.8
Public	..	..	..	..	..	..	..	..	..
Private	..	..	..	..	..	..	..	..	..
Foreign savings (current account of BOP)	..	..	..	..	..	..	..	..	..
Central government finances (% of GDP)									
Tax revenue (% of GDP)	10.8	9.2	10.8	8.6	14.9	12.6	14.5	4.9	..
Curr. revenue excluding grants - Taxes (% of GDP)	2.6	3.2	3.3	2.5	..	3.1	2.3	0.6	..
Current expenditure (as % of GDP)	15.3	14.9	14.7	12.8	..	18.8	19.7	..	..
Wages and salaries (% of total expenditure)	10.8	9.8	12.6	11.5	..	..	21.2	..	..
Subsidies & other cur. transfers (% of tot. exp.)	43.0	40.0	38.0	37.9	..	8.6	18.5	..	..
Interest payments (% of GDP)	3.7	4.3	4.5	..	..	26.7	24.1	..	..
Capital expenditure (% of GDP)	1.9	1.9	1.7	1.0	..	2.8	5.0	..	..
Primary deficit/surplus (as % of GDP; ES; GOI)	4.0	2.7	1.3	1.5	..	..	..	..	..
Overall budget deficit, including grants (% of GDP)	-8.1	-7.5	-7.8	-5.2	-10.4	-6.3	-8.0	-1.6	-5.6
Role of government and institutional quality									
State-owned enterprises (SOE), economic activity (% of GDP)	13.0	14.7	..	..	..	..	..	..	..
SOE investment (% of GDI)	32.2	32.7	..	..	..	32.5	..	19.2	..
Military expenditure (% of GNP)	2.9	2.7	2.4	..	..	6.1	4.6	2.3	..
Transparency International corruption index	..	..	2.8	..	..	2.5	..	2.9	..
ICRG: Risk rating, composite (scale...)	..	..	..	..	..	..	..	..	..
Law and order index	..	..	4 [B]	4 [B]	4 [B]	3 [B]	3 [B]	4 [B]	..
Corruption index	..	..	3 [B]	3 [B]	3 [B]	2 [C]	4 [A]	1 [C]	..
Bureaucratic quality index	..	..	3 [A]	3 [A]	3 [A]	2 [B]	2 [B]	2 [B]	1.0
World Competitiveness Yearbook (decile rank out of 46 countries)	..	9th	9th			..	..	6th	..
of which: WCY Government	..	9th	10th			..	..	2nd	..
Heritage government intervention index[a]	..	..	3 [B]	4 [B]	3 [B]	3 [B]	2 [C]	4 [A]	..
Heritage regulation index[a]	..	..	4 [C]	4 [B]	4 [B]	4 [B]	3 [C]	4 [B]	..
Heritage wage and price control index[a]	..	..	4 [C]	4 [A]	4 [A]	3 [B]	2 [C]	3 [B]	..
Highest marginal tax rate, individual	..	..	33	..	..	..	30	45	..
Highest marginal tax rate, corporate (%)	..	..	35	..	..	..	35	30	..
"Institutional Investor" credit rating (scale...)	..	..	..	..	..	..	..	..	..
"Euromoney" creditworthiness rating[a]	..	..	..	51.8 [A]	52.6 [A]	30.9 [C]	41.4 [B]	57.6 [A]	..
"Moody's LT foreign currency debt rating	..	..	..	Ba 2	Ba2	Caa 1	..	A3	..
"Dunn & Brad Street" risk rating	..	..	..	DB3c	DB3c	DB5c	DB4d	DB3a	

Note: Latest single year when available. $ = US dollar.

a. A: High outlier B: Medium C: Low outlier

Source: *World Development Indicators* (World Bank, 1999), Heritage Foundation, *World Competitiveness Yearbook* (1997), *International Country Risk Guide,* *Comprehensive Development Review* (6/30/99).

Table A.1: Economic and Social Indicators for India and Selected Comparators (continued)

D. FINANCIAL SECTOR AND GLOBAL LINKS	India 1986-90	India 1991-93	India 1994-97	India 1998	India 1999	Pakistan 1994-99	Sri Lanka 1994-99	China 1994-99	Low income 1994-99
Financial sector									
Financial depth (M2, % of GDP)	42.4	45.0	47.8	44.3		44.4	29.8	124.3	..
Real interest rate (%)	5.0	6.2	7.9	4.3	6.7	..	-2.6	7.5	..
Dom. credit provided by banking sector (% of GDP)	54.7	52.6	49.7	45.1	44.9	47.0	31.9	130.4	42.5
Credit to private sector (% of GDP)	26.8	25.8	25.7	..		..	..	..	..
Market capitalization of listed co.s (US$ b.)	38.6	98.0	128.5	105.2	184.6	6.9	1.6	330.7	268.1
Listed domestic companies, total	6,200	6,800	8,800	5,860	5,863	765	239	950	8,332
Interest rate spread (lending rate minus LIBOR)	8.19	13.0	8.1	8.0	..	..	0.4	0.8	
Interest rate spread (lending rate minus deposit rate)	..	..	..	..	..	..	-7.0	3.6	-4.8
Heritage banking index [A=High outlier, C=low [2]	..	..	4 [C]	4 [A]	4 [A]	3 [B]	3 [B]	4 [A]	..
Openness									
Trade share of GDP (%)	18.3	23.0	27.1	24.8	25.0	34.1	78.4	41.7	45.8
Terms of Trade (1987=100)	110.0	114.7	94.8	89.1		105.6	106.2	101.5	..
Mean tariff (% of all products)	81.8		30.0			..	20.0	17.6	..
Manufactures exports (% of merchandise exports)	70.7	73.8	73.5	..	77.6	68.9	72.5	88.9	76.7
Heritage trade policy index [a]	..	..	5 [C]	5 [A]	5 [A]	5 [A]	3 [C]	5 [A]	..
Heritage foreign investment index [a]			3 [B]	4 [A]	4 [A]	3 [B]	3 [B]	4 [A]	..
Current account balance (BoP, current US $ b.)	-10.3	-1.9	-5.8	-4.9	-9.2	-1.6	-0.28	29.3	4.9
Official exchange rate (LCU per US$, period average)	17.5	30.5	36.3	41.3	43.1	49.1	70.4	8.3	..
Real effective exchange rate index (1990 = 100)	100.0	71.5	76.1	73.3		91.4	119.3	106.9	..
Black market premium (%; Pick' Currency Y.B.) [a]	9.6	4.6		..	..	8.3	9.8	73.9	..
Debt, aid, and financial flows									
Total external debt stock (US$m.)	83,717	94,524	94,404	98,232	..	29,665	7,638	146,697	387,326
External debt, present value (% of GNP)	28.5	37.1	24.9		..	47.5	81.2	16.6	47.6
Multilateral debt (% of total external debt)	26.0	29.4	31.2	31.1	..	40.1	37.7	12.9	30.1
Concessional debt (% of total external debt)	46.3	45.2	41.2	41.3	..	50.3	79.5	12.3	44.9
Short-term debt (% of total external debt)	10.2	3.8	5.3	4.4	..	8.4	6.3	21.4	10.8
Aggregate net resource flows & Transfers (US$ m.)	4,719	7,264	6,918	7,604	..	3,058	984	65,370	90,500
Debt outstanding (US$m.)	72,550	85,676	88,694	93,616	..	25,902	6,725	115,233	..
Net flows on debt (US$m)	3,940	4,388	682	4,151	..	1,935	338	12,449	..
Official creditors (US$m.)	2,334	1,755	-312		..	803	292	4,315	..
Private creditors (US$m.)	1,710	2,069	953		..	790	54	6,823	..
Grants, exc. tech. cooperation (DRS, cur. US$ m.)	512	485	543	476	..	158	118	228	14,929
Foreign dir. investment by rep. country (BoP, US$m.)	97	586	3,197	2,511	..	1,106	430	41,673	..
Portfolio investment, equity (DRS, US$m.)	105	1,840	2,116	1,742	..	252	98	8,457	2,373
Short-term debt (% of Gross international reserves)	151.6	24.7	17.8		..	138.2	23.5	21.5	..
Total debt service (% of exports)	31.4	26.6	19.6	17.7	..	35.2	6.4	8.6	16.9
Aid (% of central government expenditures)	2.6	3.3	2.6	2.5	..	8.0	12.5	4.1	..
Aid (% of GNP)	0.5	0.6	0.4	0.4	..	1.7	3.2	0.3	1.3
Aid (% of gross domestic investment)	1.8	2.6	1.8	1.6	..	9.7	12.3	0.6	4.3
Gross international reserves ($m.)	5.6	14.7	28.4	30.6	32.7	1.5	1.6	157.8	234.6
Gross international reserves (months of imports)	1.9	5.0	5.4	5.7	5.5	1.4	3.4	9.7	6.4
Net aid from Dev. Assistance Commt. members and official lenders ($m.)									
Asian Development Bank (1995)	..	..	250.0	..		315.0	79.0	511.0	1,660.0
Japan (1997)	..	..	491.8	..		92.2	134.6	576.9	2,228.0
Denmark (1997)	..	..	34.4	..		-2.7	1.5	13.7	522.0
UK (1997)	..	..	154.0	..		42.5	17.4	46.2	906.0
UN System (1997)	..	..	122.5	..		59.4	27.9	111.9	2471.0
World Bank (included in Net Flows on Debt, above)	..	..	301.8	..		474.7	61.9	1,897.9	3576.0
Total	..	..	930.2	..		449.7	232.5	1,147.8	5,316.0
World Bank flows (cumulatives of each period in $m.)									
IBRD flows									
a. Gross commitments	633.8	681.8	1085.6	400.0	93.4.3	1,646.0	0.0	9,221.0	..
b. Gross disbursements	79.6	70.4	146.3	359.5	749.2	1,445.0	0.0	5,686.2	..
c. Principal repayments	554.2	222.4	939.4	517.4	1164.7	830.6	26.8	1,359.8	..
d. Net flows (b-c)	-474.6	-152.1	-793.1	-157.8	-415.5	614.4	-26.8	4,326.4	..
e. Interest payments and fees	10.9	0.0	0.0	292.9	506.6	635.6	17.4	1,827.9	..
g. Net transfers (d-e)	-485.5	-152.1	146.3	-450.7	-922.1	-21.2	-44.2	2,498.5	..
IDA flows									
a. Gross commitments	711.7	368.7	323.2	326.7	866.4	922.2	323.2	2,250.0	..
b. Gross disbursements	402.3	391.5	366.1	588.0	948.9	1,085.6	366.1	3,014.8	..
c. Principal repayments	7.2	17.1	34.4	171.3	336.0	146.3	34.4	68.0	..
d. Net flows (b-c)	395.1	374.4	331.7	416.6	612.9	939.4	331.7	2,946.8	..
e. Interest payments and Fees	25.8	23.3	42.3	75.3	140.4	95.0	42.3	198.7	..
g. Net transfers (d-e)	369.3	351.1	289.4	341.4	472.5	844.4	289.4	2,748.1	..

Note: Latest single year when available. For China, Pakistan and Sri Lanka, the available year is 1993. $ = US dollar.

a. A=High outlier; B=Medium C=Low outlier

Source: *World Development Indicators* (World Bank, 1999), Heritage Foundation, *World Competitiveness Yearbook* (1997), *International Country Risk Guide*.

Table A.2: OED Summary Ratings for India

Projects closed, total

	Number		Percent		Net Commitments $m		Percent	
	FY81-90	FY91-00	FY81-90	FY91-00	FY81-90	FY91-00	FY81-90	FY91-00
Adjustment Loans	0	4	0	3	0	1,450	0	8
Non-Adjustment Loans	107	117	100	97	9,785	16,583	100	92
Total	107	121	100	100	9,785	18,033	100	100

Projects evaluated: OED outcome ratings

Satisfactory Outcome

	FY81-90	FY91-00	FY81-90	FY91-00	FY81-90	FY91-00	FY81-90	FY91-00
Adjustment Loans	0	3	0	75	0	1,300	0	90
Non-Adjustment Loans	77	79	72	68	6,997	11,745	72	71
Total	77	82	72	68	6,997	13,045	72	72
SAR Region	187	217	73	71	9,493	20,452	70	72
Bankwide	1,310	1,554	68	69	50,906	129,645	68	77

OED sustainability ratings

Likely Sustainability

	FY81-90	FY91-00	FY81-90	FY91-00	FY81-90	FY91-00	FY81-90	FY91-00
Adjustment Loans	0	2	0	50	0	800	0	55
Non-Adjustment Loans	27	55	47	47	3,284	9,733	53	59
Total	27	57	47	47	3,284	10,533	53	58
SAR Region	55	143	40	47	3,821	15,667	45	55
Bankwide	415	1,094	43	49	21,851	101,559	49	61

OED institutional development ratings

Substantial ID

	FY81-90	FY91-00	FY81-90	FY91-00	FY81-90	FY91-00	FY81-90	FY91-00
Adjustment Loans	0	1	0	33	0	500	0	43
Non-Adjustment Loans	10	41	18	36	1,514	6,129	26	38
Total	10	42	18	36	1,514	6,629	26	38
SAR Region	24	93	19	31	1,830	8,819	25	32
Bankwide	244	760	26	34	12,563	66,026	30	41

Disconnect ratio for projects closed[a]

	ARPP % Sat		OED % Sat		Net disconnect at exit	
	FY81-90	FY91-00	FY81-90	FY91-00	FY81-90	FY91-00
India	96%	85%	76%	70%	20%	15%
SAR Region	93%	86%	73%	73%	20%	13%
Bankwide	90%	82%	68%	69%	22%	13%

Aggregate project performance indicator (APPI)[b]

	FY96-00			FY98-00		
	No.	APPI	Std. Dev.	No.	APPI	Std. Dev
India	50	6.73	1.89	28	7.01	1.86
Region	135	6.52	1.85	80	6.71	1.87
Bankwide	1086	6.64	1.86	630	6.70	1.87

ARPP ratings of ongoing projects[c]

	Number	Percent	Net Commitments $m	Percent
Development Objectives Satisfactory				
Adjustment	0	0	0	0
Non-Adjustment Loans	62	94	10,488	93
Total	62	94	10,488	93
SAR Region	120	93	14,388	92
Bankwide	1,371	94	92,661	94
Implementation Progress Satisfactory				
Adjustment	0	0	0	0
Non-Adjustment Loans	61	94	10,468	93
Total	61	94	10,468	93
SAR Region	114	90	14,181	91
Bankwide	1,303	90	87,518	89

Note: Computations are based on ARPP exit FY from OED data as of August 31, 2000.

a. The net disconnect is the difference between ARPP % satisfactory at exit and OED % satisfactory outcome rating; the Region and Bankwide net disconnect is for the period FY90-97 (ARPP review).

b. See page 4 of table A.3 for an explanation of this indicator.

c. ARPP ratings for ongoing projects as of December 31, 2000.

Table A.3: Portfolio of Bank Lending to India (Exit/Approval FY1990-00)

Project ID	Project name	Net commitment US$m.	Approval date	Closing date	Outcome[b]	Sustainability	Institutional development impact	APPI[c]	Bank performance	Borrower performance	QAG at risk	Latest IP from PSR	Latest BO from PSR	ARPP exit year	% Cancelled
Agriculture															
9786	Madhya Pradesh Major Irrigation	186.5	09/15/81	06/30/91	Sat	Uncertain	Not Rated	6.75	nr	nr				1991	15.2
9788	West Bengal social forestry project	28.8	10/06/81	03/31/91	Sat	Uncertain	Modest	6.75	nr	nr				1991	0.7
9802	Jammu & Kashmir and Haryana social forestry project	33.0	08/03/82	03/31/91	Sat	Uncertain	Modest	6.75	nr	nr				1991	0.0
9798	Haryana irrigaiton II project	133.8	01/25/83	03/31/92	Sat	Likely	Substantial	8.25	nr	nr				1992	10.8
9799	Uttar Pradesh Tubewells 2	101.0	03/08/83	03/31/91	Unsat	Unlikely	Substantial	5.25	nr	nr				1991	0.0
9797	Himalayan Watershed Management	28.3	05/31/83	09/30/92	Marg Unsat	Uncertain	Modest	5.25	nr	nr				1993	38.8
9801	Maharashtra water utilization project	31.4	06/09/83	08/31/91	Unsat	Uncertain	Modest	4.50	nr	nr				1992	42.5
9812	Rainfed Areas Watershed Dev	20.1	12/08/83	12/31/93	Sat	Uncertain	Modest	6.75	nr	nr				1994	35.2
9817	Karnataka social forestry project	24.7	12/20/83	03/31/92	Sat	Unlikely	Negligible	6.00	nr	nr				1992	8.6
9814	Periyar Vaigai Irrigation 2	33.1	05/01/84	10/31/93	Sat	Likely	Substantial	8.25	nr	nr				1994	5.4
9813	Upper Ganga Irrigation	100.4	05/24/84	09/30/94	Sat	Uncertain	Modest	6.75	nr	nr				1995	19.7
9815	Gujarat Medium Irrigation 2	145.2	06/12/84	03/31/94	Sat	Unlikely	Substantial	7.75	nr	nr				1994	15.6
9811	3rd. National cooperative dev. corporation project	188.6	06/19/84	06/30/92	Sat	Unlikely	Modest	4.25	nr	nr				1992	14.3
9834	Kerala Social Forestry	25.8	07/31/84	03/31/93	Sat	Unlikely	Modest	6.50	Sat	Sat				1993	19.0
9832	National agricultural extension project	33.0	10/02/84	03/31/93	Marg Sat	Uncertain	Substantial	7.00	nr	nr				1993	15.5
9829	Narmada Riv Dev. (Gujarat) S. S. Dam & Power	118.5	03/07/85	06/30/95	Marg Sat	Uncertain	Modest	6.00	nr	nr				1993	60.5
9830	Narmada Riv Dev (Gujarat) Water Delivery & Drainage	145.2	03/07/85	07/01/92	Marg Sat	Uncertain	Substantial	7.00	nr	nr				1993	3.2
9833	Second national agricultural extension project	37.1	03/26/85	03/31/93	Marg Sat	Uncertain	Modest	6.00	nr	nr				1993	24.2
9848	National Social Forestry	154.1	06/18/85	03/31/93	Sat	Likely	Modest	7.25	Sat	Sat				1993	6.6
9845	West Bengal Minor Irrigation	39.4	07/02/85	03/31/94	Sat	Likely	Substantial	8.25	nr	nr				1994	60.2
9893	Maharashtra Composite Irrigation III	128.8	07/16/85	12/31/96	Unsat	Unlikely	Negligible	3.75	Unsat	Unsat				1997	19.5
9847	Nat. Agricultural Res. 2	57.2	10/22/85	06/30/96	Unsat	Uncertain	Substantial	7.75	Sat	Sat				1996	20.6
9828	Nabard credit project	375.0	02/25/86	06/30/91	Unsat	Uncertain	Modest	4.50	nr	nr				1991	0.0
9843	Andhra Pradesh Irrigation 2	140.0	03/20/86	06/30/94	Highly Unsat	Uncertain	Negligible	2.25	nr	nr				1994	48.3
9859	Bihar Public Tubewell	22.3	10/16/86	05/31/94	Unsat	Unlikely	Negligible	3.75	nr	nr				1994	67.2
9863	Nat. Agricultural Exten. 3	66.6	01/20/87	03/31/95	Marg Unsat	Uncertain	Modest	5.00	nr	Sat				1995	21.6
9846	National Water Management	114.0	03/24/87	03/31/95	Unsat	Unlikely	Negligible	3.75	Highly Unsat	Unsat				1995	0.0
9962	National Dairy 2	277.1	12/15/87	04/30/96	Sat	Likely	Substantial	8.25	Unsat	Sat				1996	23.0
9922	National Seeds 3	147.2	08/25/88	06/30/96	Sat	Uncertain	Modest	6.75	Sat	Unsat				1996	1.8
9898	Upper Krishna (Phase II) Irrig	166.8	05/04/89	06/30/97	Unsat	Unlikely	Modest	4.25	Unsat	Unsat				1997	48.7
9996	National Sericulture	106.3	05/18/89	12/31/96	Unsat	Uncertain	Modest	4.50	Unsat	Unsat				1997	39.9
9965	Punjab Irrigation & Drainage	145.3	12/14/89	07/31/98	Unsat	Uncertain	Negligible	4.00	Unsat	Unsat				1999	11.9
10362	Emergency Reconstruction	210.0	10/04/90	03/31/94	Sat	Uncertain	Substantial	7.75	nr	nr				1994	0.0
9958	Agricultural Dev - Tamil Nadu	112.8	03/12/91	12/31/98	Sat	Likely	Substantial	8.25	Sat	Sat	Actual	Sat	Unsat	1999	0.0
9921	Shrimp & Fish Culture Dev.	36.0	1/14/1992	12/31/1999		Non Evaluable	Substantial			Sat	Nonrisky	Sat	Sat		57.6
10390	Maharashtra Forestry	108.0	1/14/1992	3/31/2000	Mod. Sat		Modest		Sat	Sat				1998	12.9
10391	West Bengal Forestry	34.0	03/17/92	12/31/97	Marg Sat	Uncertain		6.00	Sat	Sat					0.0
9959	Rubber	55.0	7/2/1992	9/30/1999							Nonrisky	Sat	Sat		40.2
10407	ADP - Rajastan	106.0	11/12/1992	9/30/1999							Nonrisky	Sat	Sat		0.0
9961	UP Sodic Lands Reclamation	55.0	6/10/1993	3/31/2001							Nonrisky	Sat	Sat		0.0
10448	Forestry Research Ed.	47.0	2/24/1994	12/31/1999							Nonrisky	Sat	Sat		0.0
10449	Andra Pradesh Forestry	77.0	2/24/1994	9/30/2000							Nonrisky	Sat	Usat		0.0
9964	Water Resources Consolidation	258.0	3/29/1994	12/31/2000								Sat	Sat		0.0
10503	Agricultural Human Resources Development	60.0	3/30/1995	12/31/2000	Sat	Likely	Substantial		Sat	Sat	Nonrisky	Sat	Sat		0.0
10506	MP Forestry	58.0	3/30/1995	12/31/1999							Nonrisky	Sat	Sat		0.0
10522	Assam Rural Infrastructure Development	126.0	5/25/1995	12/31/2003							Nonrisky	Sat	Sat		0.0
10476	Tamil Nadu WRCP	283.0	6/20/1995	3/31/2002							Nonrisky	Sat	Sat		0.0
10529	Orissa WRCP	291.0	12/19/1995	9/30/2002							Nonrisky	Sat	Sat		0.0
36062	Ecodevelopment	28.0	9/5/1996	6/30/2002							Nonrisky	Sat	Sat		0.0
35158	AP Irrigation III	325.0	5/20/1997	1/31/2003							Nonrisky	Sat	Sat		0.0
35169	U.P. Forestry	53.0	12/9/1997	7/31/2002							Nonrisky	Sat	Sat		0.0
10561	National Agricultural Technology	197.0	3/17/1998	12/31/2003							Nonrisky	Sat	Sat		0.0
49477	Kerala Forestry	39.0	3/24/1998	12/31/2002							Nonrisky	Sat	Sat		0.0
35824	UP Diversified Agricultural Support	130.0	6/30/1998	3/31/2004							Nonrisky	Sat	Sat		0.0
50646	UP Sodic Lands II	194.0	12/15/1998	9/30/2005							Nonrisky	Sat	Sat		0.0
41264	Watershed Management Hills II	135.0	6/15/1999	3/31/2005							Nonrisky	Sat	Sat		0.0
Education															
9990	Vocational Training	116.7	04/27/89	12/31/98	Sat	Likely	Modest	7.25	Sat	Sat		Sat	Sat	1999	58.3
9989	Technician Education	216.2	05/01/90	09/30/98	Highly Sat	Likely	Substantial	10.00	Highly Sat	Sat		Hsat	Hsat	1999	16.9
9988	Technical Education II	256.0	3/28/1991	10/31/1999	Highly Sat	Likely	Substantial		Sat	Sat	Nonrisky	Hsat	Hsat		16.6

Note: This table include evaluated projects with OED ratings (176) and active projects with and without QAG / ARPP ratings (80) as of December 31, 2000. nr: not rated.

Table A.3: Portfolio of Bank Lending to India (Exit/Approval FY1990-00) *(continued)*

Project ID	Project name	Net commitment US$m.	Approval date	Closing date	Outcome[b]	Sustainability	Institutional development Impact	APPP[c]	Bank performance	Borrower performance	QAG at risk	Latest IP from PSR	Latest DO from PSR	ARPP exit year	% Cancelled
9955	UP Basic Education	165.0	6/10/1993	9/30/2000							Nonrisky	Sat	Sat		0.0
10464	District Primary Education	260.0	11/22/1994	3/31/2002							Nonrisky	Sat	Sat		0.0
35821	District Primary Education 2	425.0	6/6/1996	6/30/2003							Nonrisky	Sat	Sat		0.0
38021	DPEP III (BIHAR)	152.0	12/4/1997	9/30/2003							Potential	Sat	Sat		0.0
50638	UP Basic Education II	59.0	12/4/1997	9/30/2000							Nonrisky	Sat	Sat		0.0
45050	Rajasthan DPEP	86.0	6/8/1999	12/31/2004							Nonrisky	Sat	Sat		0.0
50667	UP DPEP III	182.4	12/16/1999	9/30/2005											0.0
Electric power and other energy															
9794	Second Korba thermal power project	386.5	07/07/81	12/31/91	Sat	Likely	Substantial	8.25	nr	nr				1992	3.4
9793	Second Ramagundam thermal power project	277.2	12/22/81	03/31/92	Sat	Likely	Substantial	8.25	nr	nr				1992	7.6
9805	Upper Indravati Hydro	170.4	05/10/83	06/30/95	Unsat	Uncertain	Modest	4.50	nr	nr				1995	47.8
9806	Central power transmission project	131.5	05/19/83	03/31/92	Sat	Likely	Modest	7.25	nr	nr				1992	47.5
9822	Indira Sarovar Hydroelectric	15.3	05/17/84	06/30/94	Unsat	Likely	Modest	5.00	nr	nr				1994	94.9
9824	Farakka Thermal Power 2	246.1	06/14/84	04/30/94	Unsat	Likely	Negligible	4.50	Unsat	Sat				1994	18.2
9823	Trombay Thermal Power 4	134.4	06/27/84	06/30/92	Sat	Likely	Not Rated		nr	nr				1992	0.7
9839	Chandrapur Thermal Power	191.3	05/16/85	03/31/94	Marg Sat	Uncertain	Negligible	5.50	nr	nr				1994	36.2
9853	Rihand Power Transmission	185.9	05/28/85	12/31/94	Sat	Likely	Substantial	8.25	nr	nr				1994	25.6
9838	Kerala Power	99.6	06/13/85	12/31/94	Unsat	Uncertain	Negligible	4.00	nr	nr				1995	43.4
9947	Combined Cycle Power	485.0	04/01/86	12/31/93	Sat	Likely	Modest	7.25	nr	nr				1994	0.0
9948	Karnataka Power	69.6	06/04/87	12/31/95	Highly Unsat	Uncertain	Negligible	2.25	nr	nr				1994	78.9
9925	Talcher Thermal Power	272.8	06/17/87	03/31/95	Marg Sat	Likely	Modest	6.50	Unsat	Unsat				1997	27.3
9854	Nat. Capital Power Supply	322.8	06/17/87	12/31/95	Unsat	Unlikely	Negligible	3.75	Unsat	Unsat				1996	33.4
9901	Karnataka Power 2	24.0	05/10/88	12/31/96	Highly Unsat	Unlikely	Negligible	2.00	nr	nr				1994	90.8
9920	Uttar Pradesh power project	24.4	06/15/88	12/31/96	Highly Unsat	Unlikely	Negligible	2.00	nr	nr				1993	93.0
9869	Nathpa Jhakri Hydro Project	485.0	3/2/1989	12/31/2002							Nonrisky	Sat	Sat		0.0
9941	Maharashtra Power	337.3	06/15/89	12/31/98	Unsat	Uncertain	Negligible	4.00	Sat	Unsat	Nonrisky	Sat	Sat	1999	15.7
9900	Private Power Utilities (TEC)	98.0	06/26/90	06/30/95	Sat	Likely	Substantial	8.25	nr	nr	Nonrisky	Sat	Sat	1995	0.0
9982	NOR REG TRANSM	485.0	6/26/1990	9/30/1999							Nonrisky	Sat	Sat		0.0
9993	Private Power Utilities (BSES)	195.0	06/13/91	12/31/96	Highly Sat	Likely	Substantial	10.00	Highly Sat	Highly Sat				1997	2.5
10385	Oil and Gas Sector Development	150.0	07/23/91	06/30/92	Unsat	Uncertain	Negligible	4.00	nr	nr	Nonrisky	Sat	Sat	1992	0.0
9888	Power Utilities Efficiency	208.2	01/28/92	06/30/98	Marg Sat	Unlikely	Modest	5.75	Sat	Sat		Sat	Sat	1998	21.4
10400	Maharashtra Power 2	112.3	06/25/92	06/30/98	Unsat	Uncertain	Modest	4.50	Sat	Unsat	Nonrisky	Sat	Sat	1998	67.9
10416	PGC Power System	275.0	3/23/1993	6/30/2000							Nonrisky	Sat	Sat		21.4
10422	Tech Assist(Private Power Dev)	1.2	06/24/93	12/31/96	Unsat	Unlikely	Modest	4.25	Unsat	Unsat	Nonrisky	Unsat	Unsat	1997	94.0
10423	NTPC power generatio	400.0	6/29/1993	9/30/1998	Sat	Likely	Substantial		Sat	Sat	Nonrisky	Unsat	Unsat		0.0
35170	Orissa Power Sector	350.0	5/14/1996	12/31/2002							Nonrisky	Usat	Usat		0.0
35160	Haryana Power APL-I	60.0	1/15/1998	12/31/2000							Nonrisky	Usat	Usat		0.0
49537	AP Power APL I	210.0	2/18/1999	8/31/2003							Nonrisky	Sat	Sat		0.0
35172	UP Power Sector Restructuring Project	150.0	4/25/2000	12/31/2004							Nonrisky	Sat	Sat		0.0
49770	Renewable Energy II	130.0	6/22/2000	3/31/2006							Nonrisky	Sat	Sat		0.0
Environment															
9860	Watershed Management Plains	55.0	5/15/1990	3/31/1998	Sat	Likely	Substantial				Nonrisky	Sat	Sat	1998	0.0
9882	Watershed Management Hills	13.0	3/6/1990	6/30/1997	Sat	Likely	Substantial				Nonrisky	Sat	Sat	1996	0.0
9877	Dam Safety	93.0	5/14/1991	9/30/1999	Marg Sat	Uncertain	Modest		Sat	Sat	Nonrisky	Usat	Unsat	1997	0.0
10463	Industrial Pollution Prevention	166.0	7/26/1994	3/31/2002							Actual	Unsat	Unsat		39.2
10485	Hydrology Project	142.0	8/22/1995	3/31/2002							Nonrisky	Sat	Sat		1.2
43728	Environmental Capacity Building TA	50.0	12/23/1996	6/30/2003							Potential	Sat	Sat		0.0
Finance															
9850	Industrial Export Engineering Products	244.8	10/29/85	06/30/92	Sat	Likely	Substantial	8.25	nr	nr				1992	2.1
9991	Export Development	187.3	05/12/89	03/31/96	Unsat	Unlikely	Modest	4.25	Sat	Sat				1996	36.5
9956	Electronics Industry Development	79.1	06/15/89	03/31/97	Sat	Likely	Substantial	8.25	Sat	Sat				1997	62.3
9895	Industrial Technology Deve.	166.9	09/12/89	12/31/97	Highly Sat	Likely	Substantial	10.00	Highly Sat	Highly Sat				1998	16.6
10563	Financial Sector Development	450.0	3/23/1995	10/31/2002							Nonrisky	Sat	Sat		35.7
39935	ILFS-Infrastructure Finance	205.0	3/28/1996	9/30/2001							Nonrisky	Sat	Sat		0.0
Industry															
9819	Madhya Pradesh fertilizer project	165.7	05/17/84	06/30/92	Highly Sat	Likely	Substantial	10.00	nr	nr				1992	18.6
9836	Maharashtra Petrochemical	300.0	03/19/85	09/30/91	Sat	Likely	Substantial	8.25	nr	nr				1992	0.0
9914	Cement Industry	196.5	03/20/86	06/30/94	Sat	Likely	Substantial	8.25	Sat	Sat				1994	1.8

Note: This table include evaluated projects with OED ratings (176) and active projects with and without QAG / ARPP ratings (80) as of December 31, 2000. nr: not rated.

Table A.3: Portfolio of Bank Lending to India (Exit/Approval FY1990-00)

Project ID	Project name	Net commitment US$m.	Approval date	Closing date	Outcome[b]	Sustainability	Institutional development impact	APPR[c]	Bank performance	Borrower performance	QAG at risk	Latest IP from PSR	Latest DO from PSR	ARPP exit year	% Cancelled
9949	Cooperative Fertilizer Ind.	256.9	06/26/86	06/30/93	Sat	Likely	Modest	7.25	nr	nr				1993	15.0
9985	Industrial Fin & Tech Assist	311.9	03/31/88	12/31/95	Unsat	Unlikely	Modest	4.25	Unsat	Sat				1995	13.4
9981	Cement Industry Restructuring	273.8	05/15/90	06/30/97	Sat	Likely	Substantial	8.25	Highly Sat	Highly Sat				1997	8.7
9885	Petrochemicals Develop 2	157.3	09/13/90	03/31/98	Sat	Likely	Substantial	8.25	Sat	Sat				1998	35.8
9906	Industrial Pollution Control Project	84.0	9/31/92	6/30/1998	Marg Unsat	Uncertain	Modest	8.25	Unsat	Unsat	Nonrisky	Sat	Sat	2000	10.0
10410	Renewable Resources	190.0	12/17/1992	12/31/1999	Highly Sat										0.0
Mining															
9820	Dudhichua Coal	100.2	03/20/84	03/31/93	Sat	Likely	Substantial	8.25	nr	nr				1993	33.6
9837	Jharia Coking Coal	55.3	03/07/85	12/31/92	Unsat	Uncertain	Modest	4.50	nr	nr				1993	77.7
9868	Coal (Mining & Quality Imp.)	300.3	04/21/87	09/30/95	Sat	Likely	Negligible	6.75	Unsat	Sat	Nonrisky	Sat	Sat	1996	11.7
10411	Jharia Mine Fire Control	7.9	12/17/92	09/30/97	Marg Unsat	Uncertain	Substantial	6.25	Sat	Unsat	Nonrisky	Sat	Sat	1998	34.3
43310	Coal, Environmental & Social sector Mitigation	63.0	5/16/1996	6/30/2001							Actual	Unsat	Unsat		0.0
9979	Coal Sector Rehabilitation	517.0	9/9/1997	6/30/2003											2.8
Multisector															
10389	Structural Adjustment	500.0	12/05/91	12/31/92	Sat	Uncertain	Substantial	7.75	nr	nr	Nonrisky	Sat	Hsat	1993	0.0
9907	External Sector Adj.	300.0	06/24/93	12/31/93	Highly Sat	Likely	Not Rated		nr	nr	Nonrisky	Sat	Sat	1994	0.0
59501	Technical Assistance for Economic Reform	45.0	05/12/00	12/31/00											
65471	UP Fiscal Reform & Public Sector Restructuring	251.3	4/25/2000	12/31/05											
Oil and gas															
9818	Cambay Basin petroleum project	213.5	03/29/84	10/31/92	Highly Sat	Likely	Negligible	8.50	nr	nr				1993	12.0
9952	Oil India Petroleum	138.5	03/10/87	09/30/94	Highly Sat	Likely	Substantial	10.00	nr	nr				1995	1.1
9896	Western Gas Development	283.3	02/02/88	06/30/94	Sat	Likely	Negligible	6.75	nr	Sat				1993	4.0
9986	Petroleum Transport	43.6	04/27/89	06/30/95	Sat	Likely	Modest	7.25	Sat	Sat	Nonrisky	Sat	Sat	1995	87.2
10381	Gas Flaring Reduction	450.0	06/25/91	12/31/97	Marg Sat	Likely	Modest	6.50	Unsat	Sat				1998	0.0
Population, health, and nutrition															
9821	Third population project (Kerala and Karnataka)	54.0	12/13/83	03/31/92	Sat	Uncertain	Modest	6.75	nr	nr				1992	22.8
9852	Fourth population project	37.6	07/23/85	03/31/94	Sat	Uncertain	Modest	6.75	nr	nr				1994	26.3
9887	(Bombay & Madras) Populat. 5	51.8	06/21/88	03/31/96	Sat	Likely	Substantial	8.25	Sat	Sat	Nonrisky	Sat	Sat	1996	9.1
9910	Population 6	69.9	06/29/89	05/31/97	Sat	Likely	Modest	7.25	Sat	Sat	Nonrisky	Sat	Sat	1997	43.9
9940	Population 7	64.0	05/17/90	06/30/98	Sat	Likely	Modest	7.25	Sat	Sat	Nonrisky	Sat	Sat	1998	33.9
9932	Tamil Nadu Integated Nutrition 2	66.0	06/14/90	12/31/97	Marg Sat	Uncertain	Modest	6.00	Sat	Unsat	Nonrisky	Sat	Sat	1998	31.1
10361	Integrated Child Development Services	74.3	09/04/90	12/31/97	Marg Sat	Likely	Modest	5.00	Unsat	Unsat	Nonrisky	Sat	Sat	1998	29.9
10387	Child Survival and Safe Motherhood	214.5	09/17/91	09/30/96	Marg Sat	Likely	Modest	6.50	Sat	Sat	Nonrisky	Sat	Sat	1997	0.0
10393	National AIDS Prevention & Control Project	139.8	03/31/92	09/30/97	Sat	Likely	Substantial		Highly Sat	Sat					
9963	Population VIII	79.0	6/18/1992	6/30/2001							Nonrisky	Sat	Sat		0.0
9977	ICDS II (BIHAR & MP)	194.0	3/9/1993	9/30/2000							Nonrisky	Sat	Sat		0.0
10424	National Leprosy Elimination	76.0	6/29/1993	3/31/2000							Nonrisky	Sat	Sat		10.6
10455	Blindness Control	118.0	5/12/1994	6/30/2001							Nonrisky	Sat	Sat		0.0
10457	Population IX	89.0	6/16/1994	12/31/2001							Nonrisky	Sat	Sat		0.0
10489	AP 1ST Referral Health System	133.0	12/1/1994	3/31/2002							Nonrisky	Sat	Sat		0.0
35825	State Health Systems II	350.0	3/21/1996	3/31/2002							Nonrisky	Sat	Sat		0.0
10473	Tuberculosis Control	142.0	1/30/1997	12/31/2002							Actual	Usat	Usat		0.0
10531	Reproductive Health	248.0	5/28/1997	3/31/2003							Nonrisky	Sat	Sat		0.0
10511	Malaria Control	165.0	6/12/1997	3/31/2003							Nonrisky	Sat	Sat		0.0
10496	Orissa Health Systems	76.0	6/29/1998	3/31/2004							Actual	Usat	Usat		0.0
35827	Women & Child Development	300.0	6/29/1998	9/30/2003							Nonrisky	Sat	Sat		0.0
50651	Maharashstra Health Systems	134.0	12/8/1998	3/31/2005							Nonrisky	Sat	Sat		0.0
45051	2ND National AIDS/HIV	191.0	6/15/1999	7/31/2004							Nonrisky	Sat	Sat		0.0
67330	Immunization Strengthening Project	142.6	4/25/2000	6/30/2004							Nonrisky	Sat	Sat		0.0
50657	UP Health System Dev. Project	110.0	4/25/2000	12/31/2005							Nonrisky	Sat	Sat		0.0
Social sector /protection															
9987	Social Safety Nets	500.0	12/17/92	08/31/94	Marg Sat	Likely	Negligible	6.00	Unsat	Sat	Nonrisky	Sat	Sat	1995	0.0
44449	Rural Women's Development	20.0	3/27/1997	12/31/2003							Nonrisky	Sat	Sat		0.0
49385	AP Economic Reconstruction	543.0	6/25/1998	3/31/2004							Nonrisky	Sat	Sat		0.0
45049	AP DPIP	111.0	4/11/2000	12/31/2005							Nonrisky	Sat	Sat		
10505	Rajastan DPIP	100.5	4/25/2000	12/31/2005							Nonrisky	Sat	Sat		

Note: This table include evaluated projects with OED ratings (176) and active projects with and without QAG / ARPP ratings (80) as of December 31, 2000. nr: not rated.

Table A.3: Portfolio of Bank Lending to India (Exit/Approval FY1990-00) *(continued)*

Project ID	Project name	Net commitment US$m.	Approval date	Closing date	Outcome[b]	Sustainability	Institutional development impact	APPI[c]	Bank performance	Borrower performance	QAG at risk	Latest IP from PSR	Latest DO from PSR	ARPP exit year	% Cancelled
Telecommunications															
9849	Telecommunications 9	163.2	05/14/87	12/31/93	Marg Sat	Likely	Modest	6.50	nr	nr				1994	52.7
55456	Telecoms Sector Reform TA	62.0		12/31/2004							Nonrisky	Sat	Sat		
Transportation															
9807	2nd. Railway modernization and maintenance project	400.0	11/16/82	09/30/89	Sat	Likely	Modest	7.25	nr	nr				1990	0.0
9825	Nhava Sheva port project	229.0	03/13/84	06/30/92	Sat	Uncertain	Negligible	6.25	nr	nr				1992	8.4
9826	Railway Electrification	272.3	05/17/84	03/31/93	Unsat	Uncertain	Negligible	4.00	nr	nr				1993	3.0
9840	National highway project	103.4	05/09/85	12/31/93	Unsat	Unlikely	Negligible	3.75	nr	nr				1994	48.3
9855	Gujarat Rural Roads	84.3	02/17/87	12/31/95	Sat	Likely	Modest	7.25	Sat	Sat				1996	29.5
9871	Railway Modernization 3	245.4	05/05/88	12/31/95	Sat	Likely	Modest	7.25	Sat	Sat				1996	37.1
9973	States Road	183.4	10/20/88	06/30/98	Unsat	Uncertain	Modest	4.50	Unsat	Unsat				1998	26.6
9946	National Highways II	306.0	5/12/1992	6/30/2001							Nonrisky	Hsat	Sat		0.0
10408	Bihar Plateau	117.0	11/19/1992	6/30/2000							Nonrisky	Usat	Sat		0.0
9870	Container Transport	94.0	6/9/1994	12/31/2000							Nonrisky	Sat	Sat		0.0
45600	TA State's Road Infrastructure Development	52.0	12/5/1996	12/31/2001							Nonrisky	Sat	Hsat		0.0
49301	A.P. Emergency Cyclone	150.0	5/6/1997	7/31/2000							Nonrisky	Sat	Sat		0.0
9995	State Highways I(AP)	350.0	6/17/1997	1/31/2003							Nonrisky	Sat	Hsat		0.0
9972	National Highways III	516.0	6/12/2000	6/30/2006							Nonrisky	Sat	Sat		0.0
Urban development															
9808	Calcutta Urban Development 3	81.5	05/19/83	03/31/92	Unsat	Unlikely	Modest	4.25	nr	nr				1992	44.5
9809	Madhya Pradesh Urban Dev	12.5	06/28/83	06/30/91	Sat	Uncertain	Modest	6.75	nr	nr				1991	48.3
9841	Bombay Urban Development	93.7	01/29/85	09/30/94	Marg Sat	Unlikely	Modest	5.75	Sat	Sat				1994	32.1
9856	Gujarat Urban Development	49.5	12/17/85	03/31/95	Unsat	Uncertain	Modest	4.50	Unsat	Unsat				1995	20.1
9873	Uttar Pradesh Urban Deve.	111.0	04/21/87	03/31/96	Unsat	Unlikely	Negligible	3.75	Unsat	Unsat				1996	26.0
9976	Housing development finance corporation project	250.0	03/31/88	09/30/91	Sat	Likely	Substantial	8.25	nr	nr				1991	0.0
9872	Tamil Nadu Urban Development	254.7	06/15/88	09/30/97	Sat	Likely	Modest	7.25	Sat	Sat	Nonrisky	Sat	Sat	1998	15.1
34162	Maharashtra Emerg Earthquake	216.8	03/31/94	12/31/98	Highly Sat	Likely	Substantial	10.00	Sat	Sat	Nonrisky	Hsat	Hsat	1999	11.9
Water supply and sanitation															
9810	Water Supply & Sewerage	54.4	07/06/82	12/31/91	Marg Sat	Unlikely	Negligible	5.25	nr	nr				1992	24.5
9827	Tamil Nadu Water Supply	73.0	03/29/84	12/31/94	Sat	Likely	Substantial	8.25	nr	nr				1995	0.0
9858	Ker. Water Supply & Sanitation	20.8	07/16/85	03/31/94	Marg Sat	Uncertain	Substantial	7.00	Sat	Sat				1994	49.3
9857	Bombay Water Supply and Sewerage 3	124.2	12/16/86	06/30/96	Unsat	Likely	Negligible	4.50	Unsat	Unsat				1996	32.8
9954	Madras Water Supply & Sanit.	64.3	06/17/87	03/31/96	Sat	Likely	Substantial	8.25	Unsat	Sat				1996	6.9
9890	Hyderabad Water Supply & Sanitation	73.5	03/27/90	03/31/98	Sat	Likely	Substantial	7.75	Sat	Sat				1998	18.2
10369	Maharashtra Rural Water Supply	99.8	05/02/91	06/30/98	Marg Unsat	Uncertain	Modest	5.25	Unsat	Unsat	Nonrisky	Sat	Sat	1998	9.2
10418	Karnataka Water Supply & Environment	92.0	4/20/1993	12/31/1999							Nonrisky	Sat	Sat		0.0
10461	Madras Water Supply II	87.0	6/20/1995	6/30/2002							Nonrisky	Sat	Sat		0.0
10480	Bombay Swage Disposal	192.0	7/6/1995	12/31/2002							Nonrisky	Sat	Sat		68.5
10484	UP Rural Water	60.0	6/25/1996	5/31/2002							Nonrisky	Sat	Sat		0.0
50637	TN Urban Development II	105.0	5/27/1999	11/30/2004							Nonrisky	Sat	Sat		0.0

Evaluated projects since FY93	APPI average	Standard deviation	Number of projects
India	6.26	1.94	89
Pakistan	6.42	1.80	43
Sri Lanka	6.43	1.48	26
China	7.57	1.50	68
SAR	6.30	1.80	213
AFR	5.83	1.80	525
EAP	7.07	1.75	256
Bankwide	6.43	1.89	1,579

Note: The APPI (Aggregate Project Performance Indicator) is a cardinal index, ranging from 2 to 10, which summarizes the project-specific ordinal ratings on outcome, sustainability, and institutional development impact. A project with satisfactory outcome, uncertain sustainability, and modest ID impact) corresponds to a score of 6.75 in the Bankwide portfolio for all projects evaluated since FY93 is 6.42, and the SD = 1.9. Data as of December 31, 2000.

Ratings (current):	
Outcome	Highly satisfactory, satisfactory, moderately satisfactory, moderately unsatisfactory, unsatisfactory, highly unsatisfactory
Sustainability	Likely, uncertain, unlikely
ID Impact	High, substantial, modest, negligible
Bank performance	Highly satisfactory, satisfactory, unsatisfactory, highly unsatisfactory
Borrower performance	Highly satisfactory, satisfactory, unsatisfactory, highly unsatisfactory

Note:

(a) Outcome was initiated as satisfactory/unsatisfactory, expanded to highly satisfactory and highly unsatisfactory in 1993, marginally unsatisfactory in 1994 and moderately satisfactory and moderately unsatisfactory in 2000.

(b) Sustainability and institutional development impact were initiated in 1989 on a 3-point marginally satisfactory scale, the latter was expanded to a 4-point scale in 1994.

(c) Bank performance was initiated on a 3-point scale in 1991, similarly for borrower performance in 1993; both were adjusted to a 4-point scale in 1994.

Informal Subcommittee's Report on the India Country Assistance Evaluation

The Informal Subcommittee of the Committee on Development Effectiveness (SC) met on March 16, 2001, to discuss the *Country Assistance Evaluation (CAE) for India* (CODE2001-18). OED remarked that the evaluation had been OED's largest and most complex CAE exercise, with intensive involvement from all stakeholders. OED particularly thanked the Government of India (GoI) and Management for the collaborative approach in CAE preparation. OED reported that in the 1990s, Bank assistance was timely and effective in supporting India's structural adjustment program, energy sector reforms, water resource management at the state level, and human development. While there was progress in the Government's reform program at this time, it was well below India's potential and the sustainability of the reforms remain uncertain. Moreover, there was insufficient attention to rural poverty reduction, and the gender and social gaps are persistent problems. OED stressed that an important weakness in Bank assistance had been neglecting the policy reform needs of the agriculture and rural sectors. OED welcomed the Region's agreement to link the Bank's overall lending volumes with the implementation of an effective rural and agricultural development strategy, and to improve monitoring of the poverty and gender impacts of the GoI's programs. OED emphasized that the next CAS needed to provide quantifiable indicators to measure the future success of Bank assistance in this and other areas. Lastly, OED stressed the importance of increasing the impact of Economic Sector Work (ESW), improving the country's resettlement safeguards, and strengthening aid coordination as outlined in the CAE.

Management welcomed the CAE and the lessons learned through the preparation process. However, Management questioned the feasibility of carrying out a single evaluation exercise for a country as large and complex as India and suggested that it was difficult to evaluate the impact of the many aspects of the Bank's programs given the size of the country. Management considered that the CAE simplified the richness and complexity of the issues faced both by the country and the Bank's program as a result. Management agreed with the importance of addressing rural poverty and stressed that this played a central role in the upcoming CAS. While acknowledging that the dissemination of ESW needed improvement, Management noted that the CAE underestimated the ultimate impact of the Bank's ESW.

The SC welcomed the CAE and thanked OED for a well-written and comprehensive study noting the challenge presented by the large scale of the country and the Bank's programs. The SC recognized the tensions (as outlined in Management's remarks) in evaluating the Bank's program in a country as large and complex as India and there was debate about the most effective approach to undertaking evaluations in large countries. The SC particularly welcomed the broad consultations in the preparation of the CAE and hoped that the chapter outlining feedback from the GoI and civil society would become a regular feature in all CAEs.

The Chair representing India also thanked OED for its efforts and noted that the CAE was a useful report for the GoI and was the result of an intensive consultative process. He stressed, however, that the CAE should be understood as an evaluation of the Bank's program in India and not of India's reform program as a whole. He also noted that the report was not an exhaustive commentary on the range of development issues affecting a country as complex as India and often did not convey the nuances of the country and the Bank's program. With regard to the CAE recommendations, he noted that the GoI supported the state-focused approach, including the proposal to engage poor and non-reforming states with nonlending services and demonstration projects, but that it did not wish to see the Bank concentrate its social sector lending on the focus states alone as the GoI had a responsibility in this area to all states, regardless of their reform inclinations. Finally, he stressed that the GoI objected to the linkage of lending volumes to reforms in agricultural and rural development as proposed by the CAE.

Rural Development

The SC shared OED's concerns on the lack of progress in addressing rural poverty and stressed that the Bank needed to focus more aggressively on implementing a rural and agricultural development strategy. Members emphasized that rural poverty must be tackled if the International Development Goals were to be attained. Management responded that this was a pillar of the new CAS.

Assistance to States

Many members welcomed Management's approach of focusing efforts on reforming states but also stressed that the remaining states had serious development needs and the Bank should not disengage entirely with them. Members agreed with the CAE approach that support to the poorer performers take the form of ESW and Technical Assistance programs, but supported recent shifts in the Bank's program in favor of good performers and selectivity in Bank interventions based on receptivity to reform. One member asked whether reform was a political issue in many states and whether lack of political consensus on reform had led to "poor performers." The SC encouraged the Bank to create demonstration projects through its work with reforming states to be replicated in other states. Management commented that the Bank's current support to the states included some of the poorest and most populous states in India and that

the state of Bihar was the only left in the category of "poor performers." The new CAS was addressing this issue.

In this regard, the SC also noted that the complexities in a country as large as India created a tension between focusing Bank assistance on states versus the center. Some speakers stressed that while working with the states was welcome, this should not be done at the expense of attention to the central government, which was still the Bank's primary counterpart and client.

Donor Coordination

The SC expressed concern about weak donor coordination in India as a continuing problem. While acknowledging and welcoming the GoI's lead in this matter, the Subcommittee stressed the need for the Bank to play a role and asked how the Bank planned to improve coordination with other donors. One member noted, however, that donor coordination would be far more effective if tackled on a sector-by-sector basis and given the sophisticated democratic processes in India, should be led by the GoI. The Subcommittee urged Management to immediately address the Bank's role in improving donor coordination, particularly leveraging the decentralization of the Bank's programs in India.

Economic and Sector Work

Many speakers welcomed the quality of ESW done by the Bank in India but expressed concern at the lack of dissemination, noting that only a small group of Indian experts seemed to be using Bank ESW. The SC urged Management to work with the GoI to improve ESW dissemination and ensure broader access to the Bank's work as recommended in the CAE. Some members questioned why ESW was still necessary given the capacity, human resources, and expertise available locally in India and questioned the relevance and audience for the over 200 ESW reports done in India in the past decade. Members further stressed that the CAE needed more in-depth analysis on ESW, focusing on relevance, duplication, presence of local knowledge and expertise, and selectivity from the Bank. In this regard, the Subcommittee expressed concern that only one Public Expenditure Review had been carried out and there had been no ESW on corruption and governance issues in this time period. Speakers stressed that limited International Development Association resources, the fungibility of funds, and the shift toward programmatic lending necessitated a PER at the central level. Though many members agreed with Management that it was difficult to undertake a traditional public expenditure review (PER) in a country as large and complex as India and that innovative approaches may be required, they, nonetheless, noted that a PER-type exercise was necessary. Management responded that a PER was in the work program for the coming year. Management also responded that the Bank's economic reports had addressed public expenditure issues, at both the central and state levels, although these reports were not formally called PERs. Furthermore, the Bank's engagement at the state level placed particular emphasis on fiscal performance and extensive advisory and analytical work was done to develop programs of fiscal adjustment and improved public expenditure. Management also noted that while governance was not a pillar of the 1997 CAS, it was central to the upcoming CAS.

Project Implementation Units

Many speakers expressed concerns about the enclave nature of project implementation units (PIUs) and urged Management to mainstream implementation through the line ministries in India. One member stressed, however, that the role of PIUs should be decided on a country by country basis as many line ministries did not have the required capacity and PIUs served the important function of creating a critical mass of reformers that moved development programs forward. OED noted that the India CAE had not evaluated the PIU issue in India in detail as it did not appear to be a concern for the GoI. However, OED's overall view has been that PIUs are generally found to not be conducive to sustainable institutional development though there are cases where low capacity or emergency situations warrant establishing PIUs. The Subcommittee emphasized that the Bank needed to move away from the PIU concept and build capacity within ministries.

Evaluation Methodology

Some members questioned whether the CAE was meant to be an evaluation of the Bank's program or India's reform program. Members stressed that the development paradigm was shifting toward collaborative and comprehensive (that is, Programmatic Adjustment Lending) approaches and thus, it was difficult to clearly demarcate the Bank's program from the country's program.

Process

Many members of the SC questioned the timing of the CAE discussion and the process for Board input, noting that the CAS had already been circulated for Board discussion. They wondered how members' comments on the CAE would be incorporated into the CAS. Management responded that it had been logistically difficult to schedule the CAE discussion prior to the finalization of the CAS but that the CAS had been prepared in close consultation with the OED CAE team and incorporated the lessons from the CAE. Furthermore, the CAS would be revised after the April 5 Board discussion, leaving an opportunity to incorporate the Subcommittee's comments as required.

Pieter Stek
Chairman

ENDNOTES

Chapter 1

1. See paper by Singh (1999), which provides an interesting discussion of India's unique cultural heritage and the contribution of that culture to its democratic and social institutions.

2. The following three paragraphs are based largely on Srinivasan (2001), a background paper for this evaluation, and Basu and Pattanaik (1997). A detailed and comprehensive economic history of India through 1991 can be found in Joshi and Little (1994).

3. The official national poverty line is defined as allowing a daily per person caloric intake of 2,400 in rural areas and 2,100 in urban areas, in addition to basic clothing and transport items. The rural poverty line was Rps. 274 a month in 1997, equivalent to less than $0.25 a day at then current exchange rates. The 1966–79 per capita GNP growth rate was 0.7 percent.

4. This section draws from Khatkhate (1994), Joshi and Little (1996), Bajpai and Sachs (1997), Basu and Pattanaik (1997), Ahluwalia and Little (1998), Ahluwalia (1999), and Srinivasan (2001).

5. About 60 percent of this environmental damage stems from economic losses from unsafe domestic water supplies and unsanitary excreta disposal; another 20 percent is from soil degradation.

6. This section is based largely on Joshi and Little (1996), Bajpai and Sachs (1997), Basu and Pattanaik (1997), Ahluwalia and Little (1998), Ahluwalia (1999), and Srinivasan (2001). For a comprehensive analysis of the unfinished reform agenda see the World Bank's recent economic report (World Bank 1999a).

7. For the 1990s, military expenditures have been about 15 percent of central government expenditures, ranging between 2.1 percent and 2.7 percent of GDP.

8. For example, 23 of 26 states had not regularized extra-budgetary (unauthorized by the legislature) spending in the past five years.

9. However, 19 new private banks began operations during the 1990s. The new government's reform agenda includes improving debt recovery mechanisms, reducing the government stake in public banks to 33 percent, and formulating the first voluntary retirement scheme for the banking sector.

10. Some policy changes have recently been made and more are under consideration. For instance, in 2000, state governments in Haryana and Rajasthan reduced electricity subsidies to rural users. The central government has raised prices for wheat and rice in the Public Distribution System. The government is also proposing to restructure and merge the 36-odd rural development schemes and to revamp the credit delivery system so that the funds granted to it are more likely to reach the end users.

Chapter 2

1. This section and part of the next section summarize the first four phases in the India-Bank relationship as described in a 1997 background paper by Jochen Kraske (a former Bank manager with direct India experience).

2. In July 1989, just before the macroeconomic crisis, the Bank sent a country brief to its executive directors affirming the good growth prospects of the country and the soundness of its development strategy and policy framework, with only minor qualifications. Mild warnings about the increasing stress in the balance of payments and public sector finances were overshadowed by the extensive coverage of the positive achievements of the government's policies in the late 1980s and the implicit endorsement of the institutional and policy framework underpinning them. However, in the 1970s, Bhagwati and Desai (1970) and Bhagwati and Srinivasan (1975) had already predicted a serious macroeconomic crisis stemming from the faulty policy framework.

Chapter 3

1. For example, the sole public expenditure review (PER) for the decade (1993), a costly, three-year effort, was discussed with only a small group of government officials, was never published, and had little impact. Regional staff strongly dispute this assessment, which is based on the findings of a review of the quality and impact of the India PER commissioned by OED as an input to its Bankwide PER review, and was substantially confirmed in interviews with Indian officials during the May 1999 Country Assistance Evaluation mission. Regional staff argue that this

study reviewed comprehensively not only the content of public spending but also the institutional context in which spending decisions were made; that the PER raised for the first time the issue of central government transfers and lending to the states, and the lack of performance criteria in such transfers and lending; that these issues have gradually become part of the policy debate in India; that several of the sector reports underlying the review (ports, agriculture, social sectors) were widely disseminated in India; and that the PER was discussed among a small circle of senior officials who felt that it would be easier to implement the PER recommendations if they were not associated with the Bank.

2. A recent QAG review reached similar overall conclusions but also pointed to some weaknesses—inadequate treatments of the fiscal problem, of a possible trade-off between growth and equity, and of issues related to labor-intensity of growth and employment opportunities for the poor. The panel also found poor prioritization and inadequate analysis of the "actionability" of key policy recommendations. However, the panel underscored the value of Bank economic and sector work in India, even when it may not lead to policy changes in the short term, as long as it contributes to setting the reform agenda and shaping the public debate.

3. QAG panels rate projects' quality at entry good, satisfactory, marginal, or poor on the following criteria: project concept, objectives, and approach; technical, economic, and financial analyses; environmental analyses; social and stakeholder analyses; institutional capacity analyses; readiness for implementation; and risk assessment and sustainability. The other projects QAG evaluated in 1997 were AP Emergency Cyclone, AP Irrigation III, Malaria Control, Reproductive Health, and State Highways I.

4. These annexes are published under separate cover in OED's Working Paper Series and are available upon request.

5. Donor resources directly mobilized by Bank projects fell from $2.2 billion in fiscal 1990–94 to $0.9 billion in fiscal 1995–99 (spread among 11 cofinanciers, down from 19 during the earlier period). While in the first half of the decade adjustment lending attracted substantial donor resources ($686, or about 30 percent of total cofinancing), more than 85 percent of cofinancing in fiscal 1995–99 has been for the energy and mining sectors, with export agencies providing more than half of the total (as in earlier years).

6. The Bank's internal South Asia Region took exception to such critical remarks about partnerships and about cooperation with IFC. It noted that the extent of partnership should not be judged by the scope of cofinancing only. Other factors are at play, such as a move away from large infrastructure projects and toward projects (such as in education) where various donors all finance one program directly to the government, not as cofinanciers of the Bank projects. It also noted that IFC has just invested in Orissa's newly privatized power distribution sector.

7. Of 14 donors solicited by OED, 8 representatives in Delhi responded with a written questionnaire. Most donors indicated that an assessment of the Bank's effectiveness in aid coordination was not possible because the government was in charge.

Chapter 4

1. Tables containing the evaluators' ratings of the Bank assistance in all the sectors covered by OED sector studies or CAE background papers and descriptions of sectoral assistance strategies' objectives and achievements, as well as summaries of all sectoral evaluation inputs (CAE background papers and OED sector reviews) are published under separate cover in OED's Working Paper Series and are available upon request.

2. In its comments on an earlier draft, the Bank's internal South Asia Region noted that it has an ongoing, very detailed, and meaningful dialogue on a number of issues relating to rural development and poverty reduction at the state level. According to the Region, there is no disagreement in India, at least at the policy levels, about the need to revise fertilizer, water, and power subsidies to agriculture. And the central government has been moving, albeit cautiously, in the same directions recommended by the Bank's sector work. The Region also maintains that public debate on the need to remove do-

mestic and external trade restrictions is quite healthy, with the Bank having taken every opportunity to bring this issue to the notice of policymakers in the "focus" states. In the Region's words: "For example, the establishment of the rural poverty reduction task force in Andhra Pradesh and the proposed rural policy review in Karnataka will give an opportunity to lay these issues out and discuss them with major partner states. In Uttar Pradesh and Rajasthan, the Water Sector Restructuring projects offer an opportunity to come to grips not only with the pricing issue with regard to water but also with institutional reform of water management agencies." A number of states are finally "taking water resources management seriously. Cost recovery in irrigation is no longer a controversial issue. The issue is rather one of when and how it must be phased in."

3. In its comments on an earlier draft, the South Asia Region noted that while the Bank has indeed been working closely with a few states and its sector lending has expanded in the state road subsector, the Bank continued to have a strong program with the National Highway Authority. Indeed, looking at recent lending operations (fiscal 2000) and the lending program for fiscal 2001–03, about 40 percent of the Bank's lending volume will be for national highway projects.

4. For example, in the Uttar Pradesh Basic Education project, enrollments in the 1991–2000 period reportedly increased by 67 percent at the primary level and by 74 percent at the lower secondary level. The gross enrollment ratio increased from a baseline level of 66 percent to 107 percent (including overage children), although the target level was only 78 percent. Girls' enrollment increased significantly, reportedly by 97 percent. The dropout rate decreased, textbooks were provided on a large scale and were available in classes, while 100,000 teachers received in-service training through block and cluster resource centers. Large numbers of teachers were appointed, particularly locally residing para-teachers. Instructional methodology was emphasized and child-centered methodologies were disseminated to teachers and parents.

5. In its comments, the Ministry of Human Resource Development argued that there is no merit to such questions. The Ministry's view is that, under the District Primary Education Programme, many extensive research studies and more than 250 evaluations have been made; data reporting systems have been effectively strengthened over the years; there are effective monitoring and training components for the Village Education Committee; and the elaborate joint supervision mechanism, involving donors, national research institutes, and other local experts, is very collaborative, with no question of government domination.

6. Including withdrawal of support for the Sardar Sarovar dam and a power project on the Narmada River.

7. For example, the Karnataka Rural Water Supply and Environmental Sanitation project (approved in fiscal 1993) built on lessons of a previous project in Maharashtra, which in turn led to improvements and greater investments (7 percent of project budget devoted to participation compared with 2 percent in the Karnataka project) in the Uttar Pradesh Water Supply project (approved in fiscal 1998). The state of the art District Poverty Initiative projects and Integrated Watershed Development projects, some of which have already been approved, are founded on a social development approach of empowering the poor through community groups.

Chapter 6

1. For the full list of International Development Goals see http://www.oecd.org/dac/Indicators/htm/goals.htm

2. The Ministry of Human Resource Development took exception to this recommendation. The Ministry's view is that "education, especially elementary schooling, needs to be viewed differently from other sectors. It is the obligation of the government to provide universal education up to the age of 14. The GOI's [government's] inputs to the states, particularly in the education sector, depend on several factors, such as educational backwardness and regional disparities, and the like. It would, therefore, not be appropriate to link the external funding to the reforms in other sectors."

Chapter 7

1. There were 12 half-day, sectoral CAE/CAS workshops on outreach (March 14, 2000), urban development (March 24), education (March 29), energy (March 30, South Asia presentation only), transport (March 30), private sector development/financial sector development (March 31), public sector management (March 31), social development (April 3), gender (April 3), environment (April 4), health (April 4, South Asia presentation only), agriculture and rural development (April 5), where presentations of the preliminary findings of the CAE background papers and thoughts by Bank staff on future sectoral assistance strategies were discussed by groups of 20–30 stakeholders from the central and state government and parastatals, academics and policy analysts, and representatives from nongovernmental organizations and other elements of civil society. An all-day CAE/CAS synthesis workshop was held on April 6, 2000, where presentations by OED of the preliminary CAE findings and by South Asia staff of thoughts about future Country Assistance Strategy were discussed by two panels and by a larger audience of stakeholders (about 60–80). The draft CAE (dated January 31, 2000), however, given the need for confidentiality and privileged consultations, was only shared and discussed (in additional sessions) with the CAE advisers, Bank staff, current government officials, a small number of former officials, and the CAE/CAS workshop panel discussants. All other workshop participants only had the benefit of a presentation, albeit a substantive one, of the draft CAE findings.

2. R. Mohan, A. Ray, G. Sen, and A. Sengupta. The feedback from all other CAE reviewers had already been incorporated into the January 31, 2000, draft on which the India-based advisers commented.

BIBLIOGRAPHY

Background Papers/Working Papers

Published as part of OED's Working Paper Series and available on request.

Abadzi, Helen. 2001. *Evaluating Bank Assistance to India for Education Sector Development in the 1990s.* OED Working Paper. Washington, D.C.

Aiyar, Swaminathan. 2001. *World Bank's Image and Outreach Effectiveness in the 1990s.* OED Working Paper. Washington, D.C.

Basu, Ananya. 2001. *Evaluating Bank Assistance to India for Gender Equality in the 1990s.* OED Working Paper. Washington, D.C.

Khatkhate, Dinanath. 2001a. *Evaluating Bank Assistance to India for Financial Sector Development in the 1990s.* OED Working Paper. Washington, D.C.

————. 2001b. *Evaluating Bank Assistance to India for Private Sector Development in the 1990s.* OED Working Paper. Washington, D.C.

Levy, Hernan. 2001. *Evaluating Bank Assistance to India for Transport Sector Development in the 1990s.* OED Working Paper. Washington, D.C.

Mathur, Om Prakash. 2001. *Evaluating Bank Assistance to India for Urban Development in the 1990s.* OED Working Paper. Washington, D.C.

Pitman, G.K. 2001. *World Bank Assistance for Water Resource Management.* OED Working Paper. Washington, D.C.

Ringskog, Klas, and Nola Chow. 2001. *Evaluating Bank Assistance to India for Environmental Sustainability in the 1990s.* OED Working Paper. Washington, D.C.

Sahgal, Vinod, and Deepa Chakrapani. 2001. *Evaluating Bank Assistance for Public Financial Accountability in India in the 1990s.* OED Working Paper. Washington, D.C.

Srinivasan, T.N. 2001. *India's Development in the Near Term: Constraints and Prospects.* OED Working Paper. Washington, D.C.

Tuncer, Baran. 2001. *Evaluating Bank Assistance to India for Public Sector Management in the 1990s.* OED Working Paper. Washington, D.C.

van Holst Pellekaan, Jack. 2001a. *Evaluating Bank Assistance to India for Agricultural and Rural Development in the 1990s.* OED Working Paper. Washington, D.C.

————. 2001b. *Evaluating Bank Assistance to India for Poverty Reduction in the 1990s.* OED Working Paper. Washington, D.C.

Van Wicklin, Warren. 2001. *Evaluating Bank Assistance to India for Social Development.* OED Working Paper. Washington, D.C.

Zanini, Gianni. 2001. *India CAE: Overview of Sectoral Assistance Evaluations.* OED Working Paper. Washington, D.C.

References

Ahluwalia, Isher Judge, and I.M.D. Little, eds. 1998. *India's Economic Reforms and Development: Essays for Manmohan Singh.* New York: Oxford University Press.

Ahluwalia, Montek. 1999. "India's Economic Reforms: An Appraisal." National Planning Commission, New Delhi.

Bajpai, Nirupam, and Jeffrey Sachs. 1997. "India's Economic Reforms: Some Lessons From East Asia." *Journal of International Trade and Economic Development* 6 (2): 135–64.

Basu, Kaushik, and Prasanta Pattanaik. 1997. "India's Economy and the Reforms of the 1990s: Genesis and Prospect." *The Journal of International Trade and Economic Development* 6 (2): 123–33.

Bhagwati, Jagdish. 1998. "The Design of Indian Development." In I.J. Ahluwalia and I.M.D. Little, eds., *India's Economic Reforms and Development: Essays for Manmohan Singh.* New York: Oxford University Press.

Bhagwati, Jagdish, and Padma Desai. 1970. *India: Planning for Industrialization.* New York: Oxford University Press.

Bhagwati, Jagdish, and T.N. Srinivasan. 1975. *Foreign Trade Regime and Economic Development: India.* New York: National Bureau of Economic Research and Columbia University Press.

Bhalla, Surjit S. 2000. *Trends in World Poverty—Ideology and Research.* New Delhi: Oxus Research and Investments.

Brandon, C., and K. Hommann. 1995. "The Cost of Inaction: Valuing the Economy-Wide Cost of Environmental Degradation in India." Paper presented at the Modeling Global Sustainability Conference, United Nations University, Tokyo, October.

Datt, Gaurav. 1999. *Has Poverty in India Declined During the Post-reform Period?* Washington, D.C.: International Food Policy Research Institute.

———. 1997. *Poverty in India 1951–1994: Trends and Decomposition.* Washington, D.C.: World Bank and International Food Policy Research Institute.

Datt, Gaurav, and Martin Ravallion. 1998. "Why Have Some Indian States Done Better than Others at Reducing Rural Poverty?" *Economica* 65 (February): 17–38.

Deaton, Angus, and Alessandro Tarozzi. 1999. "Prices and Poverty in India." Research Program in Development Studies, Princeton University, Princeton, N.J.

Easterly, William. 1997. *The Ghost of Financing Gap.* World Bank Policy Research Working Paper 1807. Washington, D.C.

Fisher, Thomas, Vijay Mahajan, and Ashok Singha. 1997. *The Forgotten Sector: Non-Farm Employment and Enterprises in Rural India.* London: Intermediate Technology.

Jha, Shikha, and Vinaya Swaroop. 1999. "Foreign Aid to India: What Does It Finance?" *Economic and Political Weekly* 34 (19): 1142–46.

Joshi, Vijay, and I.M.D. Little. 1996. India's Economic Reforms: 1991–2001. New York: Oxford University Press.

———. 1994. *India: Macroeconomics and Political Economy.* Washington D.C.: World Bank.

Khanna, Partap, and P. Ram Babu. 1997. "Environmental Evaluation of Economic Growth: An Agenda for Change." *Yojana* (August).

Khatkhate, Deena. 1994. "Intellectual Origins of Indian Economic Reform: A Review of J. Bhagwati's 'India in Transition: Freeing the Economy.'" *World Development* 22 (7): 1097–102.

Kraske, Jochen. 1997. "India and the World Bank." World Bank, Washington, D.C.

Lele, Uma, and Balu Bumb. 1995. "The Food Crisis in South Asia: The Case of India." In K. Sarwar Lateef, ed., *The Evolving Role of the World Bank: Helping Meet the Challenge of Development.* Washington, D.C.: World Bank.

Lundberg, Mattias, and Lyn Squire. 1999. *Growth and Inequality: Extracting the Lessons for Policymakers.* Washington, D.C.: World Bank.

Mearns, Robin. 1999. "Access to Rural Land in India." World Bank Policy Research Working Paper 2123. Washington, D.C.

Mearns, Robin, and Saurabh Sinha. 1999. "Social Exclusion and Land Administration in Orissa, India." World Bank Policy Research Working Paper 2124. Washington, D.C.

Ravallion, Martin. 2000. "What Is Needed for a More Pro-Poor Growth Process in India?" Paper presented at the International Symposium on Development Policies for the New Millennium in Honour of Professor Kirit Parikh, Indira Ghandi Institute of Development Research, Mumbai, India.

Ravallion, Martin, and Gaurav Datt. 1999. *When Is Growth Pro-Poor? Evidence from the Diverse Experience of India's States.* Washington, D.C.: World Bank.

———. 1996. "How Important to India's Poor Is the Sectoral Composition of Economic Growth?" *World Bank Economic Review* 10 (1): 1–25.

Singh, Balmiki Prasad. 1999. "Democracy, Ecology and Culture: The Indian Experience." Paper presented at the Sardar Patel Memorial Lecture, New Delhi, October.

Tata Energy Research Institute. 1998. *Looking Back to Think Ahead.* Delhi.

UNDP (United Nations Development Programme). 1999. *Human Development Report 1999.* New York: Oxford University Press.

Vijay, J., and I.M.D. Little. 1996. *India's Economic Reforms 1991–2000.* Oxford: Clarendon.

World Bank. 2000. *India—Reducing Poverty, Accelerating Development.* New Delhi: Oxford University Press.

———. 1999a. *Assessing Aid: What Works, What Doesn't, and Why.* Policy Research Report. New York: Oxford University Press.

———. 1999b. *India—Towards Rural Development and Poverty Reduction.* Report 18921. Washington, D.C.

———. 1998. *Uttar Pradesh: From Fiscal Crisis to Renewed Growth.* Washington, D.C.

———. 1997. *Rural Development: From Vision to Action.* Washington, D.C.